THE PROCESS PERSPECTIVE

THE **PROCESS PERSPECTIVE**

Frequently Asked Questions about Process Theology

JOHN B. COBB, JR.

Jeanyne B. Slettom, ed.

CHALICE
PRESS
ST. LOUIS, MISSOURI

Biblical quotations, unless otherwise noted, are from the *New Revised Standard Version Bible*, copyright 1989, Division of Christian Education of the National Council of the Churches of Christ in the United States of America. Used by permission. All rights reserved.

Cover art: © Getty Images
Cover and interior design: Elizabeth Wright

This book is printed on acid-free, recycled paper.

Visit Chalice Press on the World Wide Web at
www.chalicepress.com

10 9 8 7 6 5 4 3 2 1   03 04 05 06 07 08

Library of Congress Cataloging–in–Publication Data

Cobb, John B.
  The process perspective : frequently asked questions about process theology /
John Cobb, Jr. ; edited by Jeanyne B. Slettom.— 1st ed.
     p. cm.
  ISBN 0-8272-2999-2 (alk. paper)
  1. Process theology—Miscellanea. I. Slettom, Jeanyne B. II. Title.
  BT83.6.C59 2003
  230'.040—dc22

                                                       2003014875

Printed in the United States of America

CONTENTS

INTRODUCTION

I initially encountered process theology as a seminary student in 1989. At first the ideas and terminology were strange, and keeping them in mind as I read was challenging. It was like reading a novel with a huge number of characters—all of them interesting and vital to the story, but hard to keep straight. Then it started to come together, and comprehension was like landing in the Land of Oz. Whereas before, just as in the movie, everything was in black and white, now I could see in color.

These days, it seems that more and more people are seeing in color. Process theology is something that many people intuitively "get." They don't need the terminology a seminarian learns, because they already understand that God is relational, present in every moment of our lives and present in all entities and levels of being. They know that the world is interconnected, in effect a giant ecosystem where what harms one, harms all. They may have heard of the "butterfly effect," wherein the movement of a butterfly's wings in California produces rains a month later in Minnesota. Some—survivors of evil, often—have even ventured to believe in a God who is not all-powerful, not following some inexorable divine plan, but dynamically involved with the whole universe. They see God as persuading everything from the level of subatomic particles to human beings to make choices that encourage the well-being of creation—a creation not finished, but unfolding adventurously every moment of every day.

The man who has taught many to see God and the world in the colors of process theology is John B. Cobb, Jr., professor emeritus, of Claremont School of Theology. Cobb taught process theology to generations of seminary students and, as the writer of numerous books, has contributed significantly to introducing process thought to the general public as well. A theologian passionately concerned with the church and an empowered laity, Cobb many years ago also began writing for those people who intuitively "get" process theology and want to know more but who are not seminary students. They want a language that expresses what they feel but is not so technical that it becomes a barrier. In a series of books written for everyday people of faith, Cobb has sought to put process ideas into plain language, with clear implications for faithful living.

In addition to his many books, Cobb has responded to questions posed to him over the Internet, and that is the source of most of what follows in this book. For the past several years, following an initial suggestion by Cobb's friend Nelson Stringer, people have been able ask Cobb about process theology by posting questions on the Web site of Process and Faith (*www.processandfaith.org*). Process and Faith is an organization founded in 1983 by people, Cobb among them, determined to explore in nonacademic terms the application of process theology to all aspects of faith life—in worship and liturgy, religious education, biblical study, pastoral care, spiritual formation, and interfaith dialogue. It was Stringer, designer of the site, who asked Cobb if he would be willing, in the spirit of this interactive medium, to take whatever questions folks were moved to ask. Cobb agreed, and the best of those results are what you see in this book.

Of course, given that explanation, it is clear that these are not technically "frequently asked questions." They are one-time questions posed by individuals. However, behind the wording of a specific question, themes emerge, and these themes *are* frequently expressed by those who seek a clearer understanding of process thought. Accordingly, you will see that questions about the nature of God are far and away of greatest interest. Questions about Christ are fewer, and have in fact been supplemented by answers Cobb has provided in other settings, specifically, in church adult study classes. Questions about faithful living are also posed, questions concerned with biblical interpretation, relationships to the church, and ethical choices in a complex world.

Given the context for these questions, it is also clear that the answers do not comprise any systematic explanation of process theology. The questions were posed month by month, and although I have sought to arrange the answers by theme, they were not written with that in mind. Cobb's aim was to write answers for the general public; he did not presuppose either a faith background or a knowledge of process thought. Instead of a primer on process theology, then, these responses should be read as answers from a process perspective to questions of abiding human concern.

How are we to understand God? What does it mean to be a faithful Christian? Do traditional doctrines such as incarnation and atonement really make sense in a world of computers, the Hubble space telescope, and microwave ovens? Must people really choose between faith and fact? In this either/or climate of scientific fact, are the choices really limited to the premodern "faith of our fathers" or no faith at all? In these brief answers, Cobb suggests a gentle no.

There is another way. And though this "way" is called process theology, it is not a set of beliefs with its own doctrines and creed. It is a basic conceptual orientation that sees the universe as creative, interrelational, dynamic, and open to the future. It does not reflect a specific denomination or faith tradition. As a distinctive way of viewing reality, it is a way for people to deepen the particularity of their own faith while opening the way to mutual respect between faith traditions. Christian beliefs seen through the perspective of process theology are like Dorothy in the Land of Oz—still recognizably Dorothy but now appearing in color instead of black and white.

A long time ago John Calvin wrote that scripture is like a pair of "spectacles" through which we "read" a knowledge of

God. I invite you to "read" the pages that follow through the "spectacles" of process thought. I cannot promise you a knowledge of God (and Cobb himself would protest such a claim), but I can promise you a fresh perspective on faith from a man of faith—John B. Cobb, Jr.

Jeanyne B. Slettom

1

GOD

Is God almighty?

The question of God's omnipotence arises for individuals whenever they encounter personal injustice and meaningless suffering. The question arises collectively when public events bring home to the public the dimensions of evil in history. The September 11 destruction of the World Trade Towers was an event of that sort. People ask why God caused this or allowed it to happen.

The answer of process theology is, of course, that God's power is not the sort that prevents people from doing evil things. God calls and seeks to persuade. But this does not keep us from committing crimes. Far from it. Furthermore, God does not even prevent people from supposing that they are doing good when in fact they are doing evil. To us this is obvious in the case of those who gave their lives in order to harm us. They were committed idealists. To others it is obvious that the United States often inflicts great suffering on people in "developing" countries for the sake of blocking the spread of Communism or making the world safe for growth through corporate investment. These are ideals to which many Americans are deeply committed and in whose service some are willing to harm others.

God does call the Muslim terrorists to broaden their horizons so that they will understand more clearly what they are doing and subordinate their limited ideals to that of the well-being of humankind and the Earth. God similarly calls Americans. God's call is not without effect, but it is not decisive. Most of what happens in the world is shaped by idolatry, that is, by devotion to lesser goods or "gods."

To many Christians this sounds like heresy. They believe that the doctrine that God is almighty is at the heart of Christian faith. To understand God's power as "only" the power of empathy and of liberating, persuasive, and empowering love, they think, is to abandon the Christian conviction that God is in total control. Many who have rejected Christianity share the belief that the Christian God is identical with the Almighty. For them this Christian teaching justifies their rejection of Christianity.

There can be no doubt that attributing this kind of power to God has been common in the tradition and remains common in churches to this day. It underlies the question: "Why did God let that evil take place?" It also underlies a certain assurance that in spite of all the contrary evidence, no matter how viciously we behave, everything will come out right in the end.

The term *almighty* has been central to popular Christian thinking. Popular thought does not draw out the consistent implications of this idea, that is, that human beings are powerless. Indeed, it is quick to hold people responsible for their actions and to blame them for their sins in spite of the supposition that God controls everything. But the point here is that whatever the theoretical problems it engenders, the belief that God is almighty is central to the thinking of many Christians.

Indeed, among the words sometimes substituted for God, *almighty* is by far the most common. Sometimes God is named the Eternal or the Creator. But far more prayers are addressed to "Almighty God." Far less often do we address "all-loving God" or "merciful God" or "all-knowing God" or "gracious God," despite the fact that love, mercy, knowledge, and grace are far more prominent in New Testament teaching than power.

Most people suppose that in affirming this attribute and singling it out for emphasis, they are faithful to the Bible. They are wrong, but this is hardly their fault. It is the result of a fateful decision made by those who translated the Hebrew Bible into Greek. These translators found in Genesis and Job extensive references to El Shaddai, or just Shaddai. This was a proper name for a god who was originally, we may assume, not identical with Yahweh. Yahweh they translated as the Lord. What were they to do with Shaddai?

To treat Shaddai as a proper name would be to suggest that a god other than Yahweh was accepted by Israel. But long before then Israel had become very clear that it had but one God. The translators solved their problem by substituting "God Almighty" for El Shaddai and "the Almighty" for Shaddai. The reader then assumes that this is a way of speaking of the same God who is otherwise called the Lord. Because of this decision, readers of the Bible are led to assume that it teaches divine omnipotence.

Was there any linguistic reason to choose *almighty*? The answer is negative. Of course to be a god was to be powerful.

But at the time the stories of El Shaddai were originally composed, the power of this god would certainly not have been supposed to be absolute. Quite the contrary. Nothing in the name even points to power. Some scholars think the most probable original meaning was "the Breasted One." The decision to emphasize power reflects theological beliefs prevalent at the time of the translation and has nothing to do with meanings in the text itself.

To this day almost all translators have followed the Greek translation. Even the *New Revised Standard Version* does so. Each time, it provides a footnote to state the Hebrew for which *almighty* is substituted, but it does nothing to discourage the reader from supposing that the Hebrew text teaches divine omnipotence. If curious readers check the "Dictionary/ Concordance" in the back and look up *almighty,* they find it capitalized and followed by *the.* The meaning provided is "God, who is all powerful."[1] References are provided to the passages in which the Hebrew texts speak of Shaddai, and there is no hint of the arbitrariness of this substitution. It seems that even the fine scholars who work together to produce our most reliable translations do not want to inform readers that the scriptures in their original languages do not speak of God as almighty.

The harm done by this doctrine has been enormous. Millions reject Christianity because of it, and those who stay are encouraged to have unrealistic expectations. They are also encouraged to think that controlling everything is a supreme virtue and to emulate this virtue in finite ways. Despite Jesus' revelation of a very different kind of divine power and Paul's celebration of God's weakness (1 Cor. 1:25), the church continues to worship controlling power and even to remake Jesus in that image.

---

[1] *New Revised Standard Version.*

Challenging the hold of this idea on the mind of the church is not a minor task. It arouses anger. But if we are faithful to the scriptures, and especially to the revelation in Jesus, we should not hold back. Process theology has particular capabilities here and, therefore, particular responsibilities.

Is God just?

God's justice is a central teaching of all the biblical faiths, but its meaning is not always clear. In the crudest sense, it means that all of our good deeds and sins are recorded and weighed and that when we die, we receive the treatment that is proportionate to the balance. That is at best a one-sided reading of the scriptures. In the Jewish scriptures, there is little thought of rewards and punishments in an afterlife, and in the Christian scriptures, where such an afterlife is important, moral righteousness is subordinated to faith, and God's justice is overwhelmed by God's love. Furthermore, in both Jewish and Christian scriptures, justice in the sense of the retribution we deserve is tempered by mercy. We are led to rejoice that God is not "just" in this rational, moralistic way.

The book of Job is the strongest polemic against this understanding of divine justice. Job has done nothing to deserve his suffering. His "friends," who suppose that he must have because God is "just," are wrong. When God finally speaks, it is not to show that Job's suffering is just but to say that God's ways are far beyond our comprehension and that it is not for us to question them.

In the gospel of Luke, Jesus explicitly opposes the view that those who suffer must be particularly guilty (Luke 13:1–5). The Galileans slain by Herod were not worse than other

Galileans. Those killed in Jerusalem by a falling tower were no worse than other inhabitants of the city. Nevertheless, the message Jesus associates with this is that without repentance, all will perish because of their sins. Clearly, God takes sin seriously even if we cannot reason back from suffering to the particular sinfulness of those who suffer.

If God provides no neat recompense for virtue and vice, what else may be meant by God's justice? It certainly means that God wants a world in which justice and righteousness prevail. But here, justice does not mean so much rewards and punishments as fair treatment of all, especially the poor and powerless. This message is consistent through both Jewish and Christian scriptures.

Turning now to the writings of Alfred North Whitehead,[2] we find that "justice" is conspicuous by its absence. One suspects that its association with rewards and punishments was unattractive to Whitehead, and he simply avoided it. Does that mean that Whitehead denied God's justice in the sense that God will ensure that all get what they deserve? The answer must be yes. The course of events here and now does not express that kind of justice, and there is no reason to suppose that this will change in another life.

Does that mean that Whitehead failed to take sin seriously? Again, the word is conspicuous by its absence, but the idea is not. The Greek word translated as "sin" is *harmartia*. This means "missing the mark." In *Religion in the Making,* Whitehead writes of a rightness in things partly attained and partly missed, which suggests the idea of missing the mark. He regards this as very near the center of religious experience.[3] In *Process and Reality* he devotes extensive time to explaining how it occurs. Technically, it is the difference between the final phase of the subjective aim and the initial aim derived from God. In ordinary

---

[2]Alfred North Whitehead (1861–1947), English philosopher who developed the comprehensive metaphysical system that came to be known as process philosophy.

[3]Alfred North Whitehead, *Religion in the Making* (New York: Fordham, 1996), 60–61.

language, we can say that the way we actually decide in each moment what we become is always influenced by God, but is also shaped by other motives that cause us to fail to do and be what God calls us to do and be.

Does Whitehead take this seriously? Indeed! Not only does every decision we make have consequences for the whole future, it also affects the divine life itself. What we do to ourselves and our neighbors, we do also to God. How we decide in one moment affects what God can offer to us or call us to be thenceforth. The possibilities and the actualities of our entire lives depend on our responsiveness to God.

What about the other question so central to the Bible? Does Whitehead depict God as seeking justice and righteousness in earthly affairs? Although these are not his words, the answer is yes. Whitehead sees God working in our history for a world in which each respects all others, in which all are free, in which the coordination that is necessary for society is effected largely by persuasion, and in which there is such approximation to social and economic equality as is possible. This is different rhetoric from that of the Bible, but Whitehead himself affirms the connection not only to God but also to Jesus.

So does process theology affirm the justice of God? Yes, but very carefully. The idea of justice continues to be bound up in too many minds with the notion that life will deal us what we deserve and that suffering must be brought about by sin. The expectation of justice in this sense leads repeatedly to disappointment. It leads also to teachings that are truly harmful. Even the statement that God wants us to practice justice can lead to punitive practices and harsh judgments toward those of whom we disapprove. It is far better to emphasize God's love and God's desire that we love one another. The justice we do want to emphasize is that which seeks to lift up those who are downtrodden and to support the oppressed. This can be expressed more safely in terminology that is free from the damaging baggage connected with "justice."

Is God personal?

The answer to this, as to so many questions, is yes and no, but on the whole, yes is a better answer than no. Of course, everything depends on what is meant by "personal." For some people, the only way God can be personal is to be very much like a human being. In the extreme case, this involves attributing a body to God that resembles a human body. Obviously, the answer must then be no. If we think of God's having a body, that body is the universe as a whole.

More commonly, it is only the human mind or soul or spirit that God is understood to resemble. Then the answer depends on how the questioner understands the human spirit. Often it is understood in a substantialist way, with the relations among human spirits, and even between spirit and body, seen as quite external. When it is clear that the questioner is thinking in this way, it is still best to begin with the answer no. God is not like another human being, only greater, when one thinks of a human being in this way. But then, from a process perspective, other human beings are not like that either!

In somewhat more sophisticated imagery, questioners sometimes are asking whether the I–Thou relationship exists between us and God. Addressing God as Thou has been so central to the Abrahamic traditions that to rule out such language would mean a serious rupture. Process theology allows and affirms its use.

But the language of I–Thou suggests an over-againstness or externality that is inadequate and misleading. In Paul Tillich's terminology it seems to imply that God is one being alongside other beings. We need to claim the language but free it from this externalistic interpretation. Paul himself helps us to do so. He says of human beings that we are members one of another and jointly members of the body of Christ. We are in Christ, and Christ is in us. The Holy Spirit is also found within. Process thought interprets this to mean that we participate in constituting the very being of one another and that the divine reality participates in constituting our being as we participate in constituting the divine reality. We are quite literally in God, and God is quite literally in us.

I-Thou language by itself does not capture this. But this is not because the relationship that process thinkers affirm is less personal. The mutual immanence of all things only makes the personal character of relationships deeper, more inextricable. Process thought in this way enables us to appreciate the meaning of some of the language of the New Testament that has previously been toned down because of the metaphysical assumptions of interpreters.

Even so, this emphasis on the immanence of God seems to some to count against the idea of God as a personal being. In human interpersonal relations, we transcend one another as well as participate in one another. Does God transcend us? Of course. But is the way that God transcends us similar to the way other human persons transcend us?

No, there are differences. Other people are spatially separated from us. The locus from which they experience the world is different from the one from which we experience the world. But God is equally everywhere. Where we are, God is there too. Alternatively, we may judge that spatial language does not apply to God at all, so that it would be better to say the God is "nowhere." In this way, God is very different from another human person.

Nevertheless, God, like human persons, is a subject who acts and is acted on. In Whitehead's terminology, God is an actual entity, distinct from all other actual entities. This does not make God any more like humans than like creatures in general. On the other hand, we suppose that some human characteristics shared with some but by no means all other creatures are shared by God. Consciousness is an important example.

As to how much further we should go in attributing humanlike characteristics to God, process theologians divide.

Charles Hartshorne encourages us to think of God as a closely unified succession of actual entities in which all the past ones are fully included in the present one.[4] Because such a succession of actual entities is just what Whitehead defines as a "living person," Hartshorne gives a clear positive answer to the question of whether God is a person. Whitehead, on the other hand, proposes that we think of God as a single, everlasting, actual entity. That is extremely different from any creature, including the human one. In his terminology, then, God is not a person. Yet much of what believers have in mind when they ask whether God is a person is present in God for Whitehead as well.

How does process thought explain miracles, and what is God's role in them? Why do miracles occur for some and not for others?

The question as to why miracles occur for some and not for others and how God is involved is an excellent one. I think process thought can throw some light on this mystery but certainly not dispel it entirely. I'll introduce my answer by saying something about what the word *miracle* has meant.

In the modern period, scientists developed a sense of laws having been imposed on the physical world, such that what occurs is exactly determined by them. This changed miracles from being astounding occurrences to being ones that violated the laws of nature, and this became the meaning of the supernatural. Many believed that there were no miracles. Others held that they occurred or, at least, had occurred at the

---

[4]Charles Hartshorne (1897–2000), American philosopher of religion and metaphysician whose work significantly shaped process theology.

beginning of Christianity. A miracle was then understood as a unilateral intervention by God, setting aside the laws of nature and acting in a way that conflicted with them.

That understanding of miracles does not make much sense today. Most of what we call "the laws of nature" is better understood, following Whitehead, as the habits of various species of creatures. Instead of absolute imposed laws, the laws are now statistical averages. The behavior of individuals is not governed exactly by the averages; still, they work well to describe what happens when vast numbers of individuals are involved. But the behavior of individuals can deviate considerably from the average, and it is never impossible that many will deviate in the same way at the same time, so that macro events will also deviate from the norm. This might well be considered a violation of a law, but in fact it simply demonstrates the statistical nature of the law.

Of greater practical importance was the dualistic assumption that physical events could have only physical causes. This meant that in principle a person's emotions and attitudes could have no effect on the health of the body. This kind of dualism lingers on in some of the sciences, but practical life and common sense have long since rejected it.

Most doctors are now convinced that placebos have some effect and that, in general, emotions and attitudes, and even meditation and prayer, influence the healing process. Few doubt that stress can be the cause of bodily problems. This "influence of mind over matter" is so commonplace that few today would think of calling it miraculous. This is a problem for some philosophies, but certainly not for process thought.

On the other hand, process thinkers generally expect the influence to be subtle and gradual. We believe that the physical processes in the body also have their causal effects that are unlikely to be abruptly overcome by psychic ones. When changes are rapid and dramatic, we are astonished, and, like biblical writers, think that a miracle has occurred.

From the perspective of process thought, we suppose that the greatest causal efficacy in most events derives from their immediate past and their closest neighbors. Hence, a major influence of a more remote event, such as the experience of the person in whose body changes are occurring, is somewhat surprising. But we know that personal experience is in fact extremely influential in some parts of the body and that its influence in others can be heightened by intentional practice and efforts. We set no limits on the possible influence except to say that it will never render all other influences negligible. We may then agree that when the influence is very pronounced and has striking consequences, a miracle has occurred.

We are still more likely to speak of a miracle when the influence is by one person on the body of another. For many philosophies, this is difficult to understand. But process thought emphasizes the interrelation of all things in such a way that this fits, even if it is surprising.

The question that has been asked is not, however, whether such things occur, but why they happen for some people and not for others. There are those who teach that if one has enough faith, all sickness will be healed. Yet some very strong believers do not experience such healing, while others, who do not seem to be so filled with faith, are healed. Similarly, the meditational disciplines recommended for healing help some far more than others. What makes the difference?

A commonsense answer often seems relevant and fits the process model. Because the outcome is the consequence of both the state of mind and the state of the body, the difference in response may come from the latter. Sometimes the bodily condition may be such that no change in the state of mind will make much difference. Sometimes the forces of healing and sickness in the body may be more nearly balanced, so that a little added help from emotions and attitudes or psychological disciplines makes a dramatic difference.

The concern underlying the question is intensified to whatever extent one thinks of God as the unilateral agent of the healing. Why would God help more in one case than another? Does this mean that God favors the one person over the other?

Process theology holds that God is already present in the healing forces of the body and is working also in the experience of the person involved. God is calling the person to that state of mind that is most conducive to healing. God's healing work in the body is more effective when that state of mind is present.

God is calling others also to contribute what they can to healing influences. This includes their attitudes, their prayers, and sometimes their touch. It certainly includes the normal help of doctors with their drugs and operations. If the healing occurs, it is indeed God's work, whether it is facilitated by chemicals administered by doctors, by exercises prescribed by physical therapists, or by the prayers of friends. It is God's work whether it is dramatic and "miraculous" or gradual and normal. But it is not as if God works unilaterally and apart from the creatures. God does not cause the illness or determine its virulence. God does not choose to heal one and leave another to suffer. If we know that God is a loving presence in all our cells and especially in our psychic life and trust God to do what God can do, God's healing work is aided. Faith is highly relevant. But it is not magic.

Can God/Christ be violent at times?

From the point of view of process theology, God is never violent in the usual sense. Central to our understanding is that God relates to us persuasively rather than coercively; God lures us to act in that way that is best in the circumstances. By introducing possibilities for such action that go beyond what the situation would otherwise allow, God expands our freedom. Violence as we ordinarily understand it restricts the freedom of its object. We think that God's loving nature was revealed to us in Jesus, both in his behavior and in his teaching.

But to say that God is never violent does not mean that God's call to us is always comfortable or pleasant. Whitehead is quite explicit on this point. He holds that each occasion receives an "initial aim" from God. He writes, "This function of God is analogous to the remorseless working of things in Greek and in Buddhist thought. The initial aim is the best for that impasse. But if the best be bad, then the ruthlessness of God can be personified as Ate, the goddess of mischief. The chaff is burnt."[5] Hence, people can experience God as "violent" in a special sense.

This "violence" is vividly expressed by Nikos Kazantzakis: "Blowing through heaven and earth, and in our hearts and the heart of every living thing, is a gigantic breath—a great Cry—which we call God. Plant life wished to continue its motionless sleep next to stagnant waters, but the cry leaped up within it and violently shook its roots: 'Away, let go of the earth, walk!'"[6] Kazantzakis proceeds to talk of God's call to animals and then to human beings, always emphasizing creaturely resistance and divine insistence. The Cry functions persuasively, not by compulsion, but its persistence and insistence can be felt as "violent."

The question is also about human violence. That God is persuasive certainly points to the superiority of persuasion in human affairs. Process theology emphasizes that strongly. Employing compulsion is a sign of failure or desperation rather

---

[5]Alfred North Whitehead, *Process and Reality,* ed. David Ray Griffin and Donald W. Sherburne (New York: Free Press, 1978), 244.
[6]Nikos Kazantzakis, *Report to Greco* (New York: Simon and Schuster, 1965), 291–92.

than a normative approach. But in human affairs, it can often be the best choice remaining. If a baby girl is about to be hit by a car, there is no time to persuade her to move out of the way. One snatches her violently to save her life. I am confident that God calls us to do that.

Does God ever call us to injure other people? Again, I think the answer is affirmative. If killing Hitler could have stopped the Holocaust and shortened the war, Dietrich Bonhoeffer was right to support that project. On a much lesser scale, Jesus used violence to cleanse the temple.

Whitehead pointed out that "life is robbery."[7] For one creature to live, other lives are sacrificed. Certainly human life involves enormous killing of other creatures. That is the kind of world we live in.

But Whitehead goes on to say that the robber needs justification. The fact that we must destroy to live does not mean that the destruction is not evil. Because it is evil, we should minimize it. Some process thinkers make the choice for vegetarianism for this reason. Many process thinkers are deeply concerned about the extent of the violence humanity is inflicting on the earth; reducing that violence is a moral imperative.

In human affairs, the goal is to order matters as much as possible by persuasion, as little as possible by violence. To act persuasively may still involve great insistence and persistence, but it will always respect and enhance the freedom of others.

In relation to other creatures, the goal is to reduce the destructive violence we inflict on them. We know now that we must do so for our own sake as well as for others, yet our violation of the earth is undercutting our own future as a species. The poor of the world suffer first, but in time we who are rich will suffer too.

---

[7]Whitehead, *Process and Reality,* 105.

So the answer is that process thinkers do not believe that a life of complete nonviolence is possible. Jesus does not model that. But process theologian Marjorie Suchocki argues in *The Fall to Violence*[8] that unnecessary violence is the fundamental character of sin. Our emphasis should certainly be on opposing excessive violence rather than on rationalizing our present violent customs and social organization.

"God is love," says the author of 1 John. How does process thought generally answer the issue at the basis of two questions: "Is love an abstract standard outside of Godself that God embodies perfectly?" or "Is love whatever God does, simply because God does it?"

This question harks back to the Realist-Nominalist debates of the later Middle Ages. The Realists, such as Thomas Aquinas, believed that human beings have some knowledge of the distinction between good and evil. God, they argued, is purely good. The Nominalists taught that good and evil have no existence in themselves. Such distinctions depend entirely on the point of view. We cannot place our preferences as absolute and then judge God by them. On the contrary, it is God's judgment that establishes what is good and evil.

Calvin was a Nominalist. He depicted God as condemning most people to hell for all eternity. To a Realist this does not seem good, but to a Nominalist, if this is God's will, then it is good by definition. The good is what God wills.

Actually, of course, a Nominalist such as Calvin tries to help us understand why this punishment of most people is

---

[8]Marjorie Suchocki, *The Fall to Violence: Original Sin in Relational Theology* (New York: Continuum, 1995).

just. Practically there is thus some concession to normal human understanding of goodness and justice. But when this explanation reaches its limits, the appeal is to the Nominalist principle. People should accept God's will rather than protest against it.

Process theology is on the Realist side. It goes farther than the medieval Realists in adjusting Christian doctrines to the central importance of God's goodness. For example, our denial that God has controlling power over events is partly for the purpose of showing that God's working in every event is for the good. The good is understood here as that which benefits creatures. And though we know there can be debates about exactly what that is, we believe that human beings can reach considerable consensus on ideas of what is better or worse for them.

The question is posed here in terms of love. The influence of the Christ event has lifted up this way of conceiving goodness and has established it as central. Most Christians believe that for God to be good is for God to be love, that is, to aim at the good of creation and empathize with all that creatures experience.

Although thinking of goodness in just this way is deeply influenced by the life and teachings and death of Jesus, we are not told that love is good because God happens to love or that love is whatever God happens to do. On the contrary, we are given examples of love in human relationships and told that the qualities exemplified there are far more fully embodied in God. We are shown love in Jesus' acts and told that those acts give us the finest clue to what God is like.

Now if we probe further as process theologians, we may conclude that our deepest intuitions about goodness and love derive from our primarily unconscious experience of God. There may be a circularity between our understanding of what is good and loving and our understanding of God's purposes. The dichotomy assumed in the formulation of the question in the late Middle Ages may be exaggerated, but for practical purposes, we side strongly with the Realists. We use what understanding of love we have in ordinary life, especially our experience of healthy parental love, and we affirm that we discern the perfect embodiment of this in God.

Other theologies, recognizing that words gain their primary meaning in creaturely relations, suggest that the application of these terms to God is analogical. Charles Hartshorne reversed this in an interesting way, arguing that the only strictly literal use of "love" is in its application to God.[9] Our feelings toward one another are always mixed and impure. Hence, to say that we love one another is never quite literally true. But God does, literally, love us. In short, we can derive ideas from observing creaturely relations that are not purely exemplified in those relations. Some of those ideas we are warranted in applying literally to God.

Process theology presents very positive images of God (God works by love, encouragement, persuasion, etc.), but are there other images too? How does process theology understand the anger of God and notions of the devil?

It is quite correct that process theology emphasizes the goodness of God. God is that which can be completely trusted. We can take this position because we believe there is a great difference between what happens in the world and in our individual lives, on the one side, and what God aims at moment by moment, on the other. Those who believe that what happens

---

[9]This idea—that when we define love fully, we do not find it illustrated in our experience in any perfect way but only find it literally true in God's relation to creatures—is implied in Hartshorne's *Man's Vision of God* and *Omnipotence and Other Theological Mistakes*. He made this point more directly in his lectures.

is what God causes to happen must, of course, adopt a much more ambiguous view of God's character.

Even so, there is a danger that the emphasis on God's goodness can lead to a somewhat sentimental view. That, however, would be false to our tradition. Whitehead writes that what God gives us in each moment, the initial aim, "is the best for that impasse."[10] The language of God's wrath can fit in here. We can trust God to direct us to the best possible, but we certainly cannot assume that the best will be pleasant or desirable!

Following Whitehead, process theologians also speak of God's drawing us toward new contrasts that involve the sacrifice of earlier assurances. To follow God is repeatedly to die to what we have been in order to rise to what is now possible.

The question points also to the possibility of negative forms of divine reality and power. Does process thought affirm divine beings that work for evil alongside or over against the always trustworthy God? The answer is no. The evil in the world is all too understandable without positing such entities. Inertial resistance to God in the natural world becomes sloth in human beings. It simply expresses how all things would be apart from God's lure. Furthermore, once there is life, there is competition for survival. This is ruthless. The few successful life forms crowd out or kill myriads of others, and at the level of sentient life, this involves suffering. God's call to each creature involves acting in such a way as to strive to survive despite the costs to other creatures. The net result is a world that grows richer in value. But this is gained at enormous cost in suffering.

Among human beings, this same tendency to struggle for survival and other advantages continues regardless of the cost to others. In us it becomes sinful, since in our case God calls us to broaden our concern and to seek our good in concert with others rather than at their expense. But we need no special explanation for our resistance to this call.

---

[10]Whitehead, *Process and Reality*, 244.

It is also striking how what is best in us can easily intensify evil. Our relational being leads us to identify strongly with a social group. "We" is central to our language and our being. The group commands our devotion, and we are ready to sacrifice for it. This is of great value, for without it human beings (as some species of animals before us) would not have survived. But when the struggle for survival and other goods shifts from the level of individuals to that of groups, it can become even more destructive. Warfare is its most dramatic expression. God calls us both to loyalty to our own groups and also to the appreciation and acceptance of other groups. Response to the first part of this call often blocks sensitivity to the second, and the consequences are often terrible.

Of course, with human beings, far more complex forms of evil arise. We can take the capacity to transcend ourselves in real concern for others and use it to aim at control of others and even at their destruction. We can even take pleasure in the suffering of innocent people. We do need explanations of these perversions, but process thinkers turn first to students of sociology and psychology for help rather than to students of demonology.

Several process theologians have been impressed by the biblical image of powers and principalities. It seems clear that social structures develop that promote evil and inhibit good beyond the will and control of individual human beings; these may well be regarded as demonic. Their emergence, however, can be explained without recourse to demons. Only if sociology and psychology turn out to be clearly insufficient will we turn to another account.

I leave the door open here. Process theology offers no metaphysical grounds for the denial of evil forces of a personal or quasi-personal sort. For example, some students have found the phenomenon called demon possession to be best explained in just that way. Although few process theologians have accepted this analysis, it is not to be rejected out of hand. These demons would not constitute a "divine" power of evil, but they could certainly constitute important creaturely powers of evil.

Process theology treats this question, like so many questions that many try to resolve metaphysically, as an empirical issue. We should not quickly accept explanations of this kind, because so much once explained in such ways is better understood in scientific terms. But we should not foreclose such possibilities if the evidence is sufficiently strong. My judgment, as of now, is that the evidence is not sufficiently strong. But I realize that this may be because I have not examined it with sufficient care.

Is divine coercion required to explain the world?

Some have argued that process theism cannot account for the remarkable order at the base of the universe, because its exact nature and universal determination point to coercion rather than to the persuasion of which process thought speaks. This raises important questions about how God acts in the world. In terms of Whitehead's formulation in *Process and Reality,* how does the "initial aim" work? Can it function to determine with detailed exactness much about the way the world is ordered?

My current view is that, indeed, it can, and the contrary impression given by us interpreters should be corrected. Whitehead spoke of a principle of limitation. The discussions of this principle in *Science and the Modern World* and the account in *Process and Reality* have different accents.[11] But the term points to the fact that only a very few of the pure possibilities are real possibilities for any occasion. Possibilities are ordered

---

[11]See Whitehead, *Process and Reality,* part 5, chap. 2, and *Science and the Modern World* (New York: Free Press, 1967), 188, 198, 199.

by God so as to effect this limitation, and most pure possibilities are excluded. In *Science and the Modern World,* Whitehead gives the example of dimensionalities other than the four of our cosmic epoch.

In *Process and Reality,* Whitehead speaks of one decision that is unilateral, that is, not conditioned by any other. This is the primordial decision that orders possibilities in their relevance to actuality. Presumably this is the act of God that establishes the limitation required for the attainment of value. At the very end of *Process and Reality,* Whitehead associates the immanence of the Primordial Nature with the determinate conditions of all actual occasions. The many remarkable features of our cosmos, including the constants, are naturally to be understood as the result of God's ordering of possibility.

The account of the divine functioning in *Process and Reality* does not focus on the way in which God functions as the principle of limitation. It is a much richer account, in which other roles of the initial aim are discussed. For example, God determines the exact locus of the occasion. Given that locus, the occasion is formed largely by causal forces from those occasions that are in the past of the locus. But because of the initial aim, the occasion also transcends those causal forces and decides how to constitute itself in relation to them. Every occasion has some capacity for novelty, some element of self-determination. Neither God nor the past nor any combination of the two determines exactly what any occasion will become.

Finally, God's working within the occasion is not limited to introducing alternatives to sheer determination by the past. It also lures toward the actualization of the fullest possible realization of value in itself and in its contribution to others. How fully occasions follow the lure is their decision.

Against this background, we can recognize that posing the issue simply in terms of coercion and persuasion has been misleading. When process thinkers deny that God acts coercively, we are opposing all-too-common ideas about God. God is sometimes depicted as causing everything to happen just as it does. Or God is thought of as preventing something from happening that persons involved want to happen. These ideas assume that God acts on creatures as an external force. All this is alien to process thought.

Instead human beings experience God as calling them to act more lovingly toward their neighbors. They find themselves resisting, but the call continues. This call is internal to us, drawing us away from our self-centeredness. It feels like persuasion.

But does the centrality of God's persuasion imply that God strictly determines nothing? Some have seemed to say this, but Whitehead does not. God strictly determines limits precisely so that value can be realized through persuasion. If strict determination is equated with coercion, then God "coerces" extensively. But this is a drastic extension of the normal meaning of *coercion*. We could also say that God coerces us into making decisions, since God's presence in our lives is the reason we must constantly decide. But this, too, is an odd use of *coerce*.

From a process perspective, it is better to avoid "coercion" as a description of God's working in the world. We should also continue to deny that God and the past, separately or together, determine exactly how any occasion is finally actualized. But certainly we should affirm that very much about every occasion is fully determined by God and the occasion's past, and that God's share in that determination is exceedingly important. That God plays a role, and that much of what God does is determined antecedently to each occasion, is surely central to process theology. We have learned that this includes the establishment of the constants that have shaped the development of the cosmos since the Big Bang, making life possible.

One source of confusion is that process thought views many "laws" as habits of particular species; these are not "imposed" by God in a deterministic fashion. This interpretation can be applied even to elementary particles. Their behavior follows from their nature. If they change, their behavior changes, and the "laws" in question change. These "laws" and their changes can be understood as, at least in part, resulting from divine persuasion.

Those of us who have emphasized this type of "law" and its statistical character have sometimes wanted to explain all uniformities in this way. It is this that has given a misleading impression of the limits of divine power. We have seemed to deny that anything is determined by God's unilateral decision. It is time to follow Whitehead more closely.

Moving from a static concept of God to a process understanding, is there not a danger of limiting God to the process and therefore getting a static understanding again?

There is often a problem with short questions from a person whose thought one does not know. One may easily misunderstand and not really respond to the concern. But the topic here is important, and I've decided to take my chances on responding to the wrong question.

One meaning of limiting God to "the process" would be identifying God with "the process." That would be pantheism. Bernard Loomer, in his later years, moved in that direction. And I do believe that pantheism tends in a static direction, although Loomer certainly would not have agreed. The problem as I see it is that there is no longer any organ of novelty for the world. If this is what the questioner has in mind, then I agree that there is such a danger. But most process theology strongly eschews pantheism.

Other forms of process thought locate God within "the process." I would put Henry Nelson Wieman in this category.[12]

---

[12]See Wieman's *The Source of Human Good* (Chicago: University of Chicago Press, 1946). Wieman (1884–1975) was an American philosopher of natural religion who was influenced by Whitehead.

"The process" here means cosmic process, and in the case of Wieman's later writings, it means "the human process."Wieman undertakes to describe that process in which human good grows. That process he calls "God." So far as I can tell, "God" then must name either the many concrete processes that fit his description or the form they share in common. The latter, of course, is abstract, and the abstract is certainly static.

Wieman thought that the future of faith depended on freeing it from any dependence on speculation. That is why he located God so completely within the process. He believed, and I think he was correct, that when one fully understands what he is saying, it is hard to doubt the reality of God. There are processes in which human good grows, and I believe Wieman has correctly identified the pattern they exemplify. Of course, that takes a lot of explanation, and alternative descriptions and analyses are possible. Phenomenological descriptions are not in fact independent of perspective. Hence, in my view, no one is completely free from the influence of speculative beliefs.

Whitehead calls his philosophy speculative. He does not limit God to "the process" in the sense Wieman does. The totality consists of "God and the world." Of course God is an instance of process, but God is an instance that is quite distinct from the instances that make up the world. I do not see that that leads to the idea that God is static.

The preceding paragraph might cause one who is unfamiliar with process thought to think that God and the world are separate. Quite the contrary: each is constituted largely, although certainly not wholly, by its inclusion of the other. God is in the world, and the world is in God. Each continually provides novelty to the other. Their mutual immanence is the reason that neither becomes static. The immanence of the world in God is the reason that, indeed, God is a process rather than a static being, as God would be if there were no Consequent Nature.

How to think of God as a process has divided process theologians. Whitehead distinguished two types of processes, microscopic and macroscopic. Microscopic processes are the concrescences of individual actual entities. Macroscopic processes are the successions of occasions. Whitehead thought of God as a single, everlasting concrescence, hence, as more like the microscopic processes he described in such detail. Hartshorne thought of God as a personally ordered society of such concrescences, hence, as a macroscopic process, more like a human person.

There are strengths and weaknesses in both approaches, and the debate continues. But I do not see that either leads to a static view of God.

If God is evolving and changing, is God incomplete?

In one sense, the answer must certainly be yes. To be complete, one might well argue, one must be completed, finished, unsusceptible to any change. In process theology, we teach that this is not the way to understand God.

But *complete* has other meanings. The first meaning listed in my dictionary is: "Having all necessary parts; entire; whole." By this meaning, God is surely complete. God is lacking no "necessary part." God is entire and whole. Another meaning is: "Thorough, consummate, perfect." In this sense too, God is complete.

There is one meaning, however, one that may be closer to what is on the questioner's mind, whereby God is not complete. This meaning is: "Concluded, ended." God is not concluded or ended from the process perspective. God is everlasting and will never be concluded or ended. Obviously, the question would not be asked if there were not a sense of God's completeness in traditional theology that is challenged by process theology. That needs to be unpacked.

Traditional theology does not affirm that God is concluded or ended in a sense that might apply to creaturely processes. But it does affirm that God's nature, the content of God's being, has always been concluded and ended. Nothing can be added to it. If that is what is meant by complete, process theology denies God's completeness. God lacks no necessary part, is entire and whole, but this does not mean that God is static. To be entire and whole constantly involves the inclusion of a changing whole. As new events occur in the world, the inclusive whole that is God includes those new events. If God did not include them, God would not be complete. In a truly changing world, a God who did not include new events would not be complete.

Traditional theology did not intend to exclude any events, or at least knowledge of such events, from God. But to avoid this, while maintaining that nothing is ever added to the primordial completeness, traditional theology has had to deny the reality of time for God. This is the central issue. Is temporal passage ultimately illusory, so that from the divine perspective, all happens at once? That is the traditional view. Process theology rejects it. Nothing in the Bible supports it, and this view threatens the biblical understanding of the importance of history and of human responsibility.

Indeed, if one reads the Bible in any straightforward way, there is no question but that creaturely events have an impact on God that is not already predetermined. The Bible speaks often of God's interacting with human beings, and of this interaction as even changing God's mind. People are encouraged to try to influence God through prayer. None of this makes much sense if God is "complete" in the sense of eternally knowing all that has been, is, and will be as already being.

The "completeness" process theology rejects is in fact not part of much popular piety. One suspects that the questioner is not really concerned for it, and the form of the question suggests that there is some misunderstanding about process theology. Process theology does not affirm that God "evolves" in the usual meaning of that term, which today is bound up with "evolution." Again, I consult my dictionary, which gives as the primary meaning of evolution: "A gradual process in which something changes into a significantly different, especially more complex or more sophisticated, form." Nothing like this happens in God. There is a gradual process of inclusion of all that happens in the created order, but this does not change the form of God. The content of the divine life certainly grows ever more complex, but this does not affect the nature of God. If God evolved in this sense, the incompleteness of God would be religiously significant and disturbing.

I may, however, have read too much into the term *evolve*. Our interest here must be the intransitive use of the term. Here my dictionary offers several meanings. The first is: "To be part of or subject to the process of natural, temporal, or biological evolution." Here the meaning depends on the understanding of evolution we have already considered. God does not "evolve" in this sense. Another meaning, however, is: "To undergo change or transformation." And although "transformation" would be misleading if applied to God, "change" may not be. It seems that the possibly correct meaning of God evolving is that God changes, and this is the second suggestion in the question.

Now surely in some sense for process thought, God changes. Because this change does not involve any change in the form of God or in God's nature or character, it is better not to use the language of "evolution." But somewhat surprisingly, even the notion of "change" is problematic. Hartshorne affirms that God changes; Whitehead does not.

The term *change* in process thought applies to the difference between successive occasions. In the concrescence of a single occasion, there is becoming, but not change. For Hartshorne, God is best understood as a personally ordered society of occasions of divine experience. Therefore, there is change from one occasion to another, and the change is always one of increase. In each occasion, God includes all that was included in the earlier occasions and more besides. For process theologians, there is nothing objectionable about such change. Certainly it does not imply any invidious "incompleteness" in any of the successive occasions. Most of us do say, therefore, in contrast to classical theology that denies any mutability in God, that God changes. God is affected by the world and therefore is continually incorporating what happens.

It is noteworthy, however, that Whitehead does not describe God in this way. Although he agrees with Hartshorne that God is continuously incorporating the new events in the world into the divine life, he does not understand this as change. Change requires successive occasions in an enduring object. For Whitehead, God is a single, everlasting concrescence. In such a concrescence, continually new prehensions of the world are incorporated in the ever-enlarging satisfaction, but there is no "change."

This ongoing debate among process theologians about how best to conceive the divine life is of chiefly technical interest. I mention it only to indicate that the accurate discussion of God's mutability in process theology is a long way from the kinds of "changes" that critics, and even some friends, attribute to us. Our claim is that God cares what happens in the world and is responsive to us. This is the common sense of most believers. Most do not accept in their personal piety the implications of divine immutability worked out in traditional philosophical theology. But they are sometimes left in confusion. Our contribution is to provide a philosophical theology that corresponds at a basic level with the presuppositions of biblical and popular theology, rather than opposing them.

Hence, our overall view is that God is indeed perfect and complete. To be perfect and complete, God must be perfectly and completely related to everything that happens as it happens. God everlastingly enriches the divine life though this inclusion of all that happens. God everlastingly responds perfectly to the ever-changing situation of creatures. This is the meaning of divine love.

2

CHRIST

What does it mean to say that Jesus is the Christ?

In the history of Christianity, the word *Christ* has had two rather distinct uses that have led to a lot of confusion. One of those uses is, simply, as the translation of the Hebrew word for "messiah." This term is a title given to one who performs a particular role in human history. That role, as the Jew today also thinks of it, would be to bring about *shalom*. A Christian might express this idea in terms of bringing about the kingdom of God.

In that sense, to say that Jesus was the Messiah sounds very strange to Jewish ears, because nearly two thousand years later, they do not observe a world at peace or a world where justice reigns everywhere. From that point of view, history has disproved any claim that Jesus was the Messiah; that is, Jesus did not fulfill the expectations of the Messiah in the way those expectations were formulated by the Jews. They are therefore absolutely correct in saying, "If you mean by 'messiah' what we mean by 'messiah,' then Jesus was not the Messiah."

Now in a sense, Christians have always known that was true. And so we have said, "No, of course, you are right. Jesus did not fulfill the central expectations contained in the idea of a messiah, but what Jesus did do was effect at a deeper level the kind of salvation the Messiah was supposed to bring." In this way Christians claim that the label "messiah" is appropriate by transforming it. That has been the argument of the church from the early days down to the present. Accordingly, there were great struggles to show how many of the Old Testament prophecies Jesus had actually fulfilled. These days, most modern biblical scholars would side with the Jews against the early Christians in the exegesis of those passages. Nevertheless, the argument was extremely important.

However, as Christianity became a predominantly Gentile religion, the Jewish meaning of *messiah* very rapidly became secondary to the word *Christ,* which is the Greek translation of the Hebrew word. Thus we need to recognize that when today we speak of Christ, we are not using the word in the same way that contemporary Jews use the word *messiah.*

At this point in the debate, I think we can agree with the Jews. Even the early Christians agreed that many of the prophecies had not yet been fulfilled, so they looked forward to something that was to happen in the future. And the prayer we most often pray is, "Thy kingdom come, thy will be done," not as if the kingdom has already come and God's will is being done on earth, but in anticipation, in hope, for the coming of *shalom*—just as the Jews do. But Jesus is so important for us and for our salvation, and for our whole understanding of the nature of reality, that we hold on to that title, "Christ." The difference is that now we transform it into a cosmic notion instead of simply using it as a title given to one who performs a particular function in history.

The universal principle of life and light, creation and redemption, which is the presence of God in all things, is what we call Christ. The redemptive, creative activity of God everywhere is what the Christian discerns as Christ.

This brings us to the problem of how we associate this Christ so closely with the historical figure Jesus. Now many Christians, including Luther, have told us we should be Christs to our neighbors, implying that the notion of Christ should not be absolutely limited to this one figure, Jesus. But the idea of "Christ" certainly gets its meaning from Jesus. It is through Jesus that we, especially as Gentiles, have any access to understanding that the universe is under God as creative, redemptive power working everywhere and at all times.

For Christians, Christ is bound up with Jesus, and I think this is not only a subjective judgment on our part. It is a statement about the nature of reality when we claim that it is in Jesus that Christ is made known, is present, and is real. In this context, it makes sense to say that Jesus is the Christ.

What is the meaning of *incarnation* from a process perspective?

We associate the incarnation especially with Christmas. That may be a mistake. It implies that Jesus was born unique, whereas our evidence for his distinctiveness comes from his adult life. It has encouraged thinking of the differences as metaphysical rather than as structural and historical.

I am not on a crusade against traditional Christmas sentiments or against their association with incarnation. The historical implausibility of the date of Christmas and of most of the stories connected with it does not undercut the beauty and meaningfulness of the celebration. A bit of demythologization can go along with full enjoyment and appreciation. But perhaps it may be worthwhile to ask what, in a process perspective, does *incarnation* mean, and, especially, how is the idea connected with the historical figure of Jesus? We can begin by noting that process thought overcomes the main obstacle in most other forms of thought to the conceiving of incarnation. That obstacle arises from the supposition that two things cannot occupy the same space at the same time. From that it follows that if God is present in Jesus, some feature of Jesus' humanity must be replaced.

If we study the debates in the early church with this point in mind, we will be struck by how many efforts there were to identify what of Jesus was replaced: his soul, his reason, his nature, his will. We may be even more struck by the fact that the councils, for all their shortcomings, steadfastly refused to accept these rational accounts. The great mystery was that God was in Jesus without displacing any feature of Jesus' humanity. This is an instance in which we can be glad that the church refused to be rational!

Unfortunately, after the last of the christological councils had ended, a process of interpretation set in, governed by the principle that something human must be lacking. The dominant view came to be that what was lacking was a human self or person, and God constituted that self or person in Jesus. This is called the doctrine of Jesus' impersonal humanity, and it came to be thought of as orthodox. From my point of view, and that of many others, it has done great harm.

For process thought, this whole problem vanishes. It is the basic nature of reality that one actual entity is present in subsequent actual entities, participating in their very constitution. However, this presence in no way detracts from the fullness of the new actual entity. On the contrary, it contributes to it. My present moment of experience is vastly enriched by the presence in it of preceding occasions of my experience. Apart from their constitutive presence, I could not be human at all.

Clearly this applies to God's presence in the world. God is present in the most literal sense in every creaturely occasion. In human beings, God is the source of novelty, of purpose, of meaning, of openness to others, of freedom, of responsibility, and of much else besides. Far from diminishing our humanity, God is the giver of that humanity. The more fully God is present, the more fully we are human.

We confront, then, a very different problem than did the Church Fathers, who had no way of thinking of how God could be genuinely present in Jesus without diminishing Jesus' humanity. What is remarkable is that despite this, they insisted on Jesus' full humanity.

We see that God is present in everyone in such a way as to create and intensify our humanity. For us, the question is whether there is anything distinctive about the way God was in Jesus.

One response is to say that there is not. The only distinctive element is that the idea of incarnation developed around Jesus and has provided a different way of thinking about God and the world. Whatever else we say, that may indeed be the most important point. The God whom we worship is an incarnate God, incarnate in the whole world. It was because of Jesus that we learned that important truth.

A second response is to think in terms of degrees. God is in all of us, calling us to be all that is possible in each moment. The more fully we answer the call in one moment, thereby embodying God, the greater the possibility for a fuller embodiment of God in following moments. The more we resist God's call, the smaller God's role in our lives becomes. Thinking in terms of degrees, it is not difficult to see Jesus as having incarnated God with remarkable fullness. He can function for us as a paradigm of incarnation.

A third response, the one that interests me most, is to reflect on how different cultures encourage different patterns of divine presence as well as the further differences that occur among individuals in each culture. This reflection leads to considering the difference between the way God functioned in Jesus and the way God has functioned in others, including other great spiritual leaders such as Buddha or Amos or Paul or Eckhart. In my book on christology, I argued that in Jesus, at least during significant periods of his ministry, his self was co-constituted by his prehensions of his personal past and of God.[1]

The kind of doctrine of incarnation process thinkers cannot accept is that which makes Jesus metaphysically different from all other human beings. For process thought, that is not possible. Nor would it be desirable if it were possible. We also think that the idea has very little biblical support.

Within the range of possible process doctrines, whether one emphasizes similarities or differences largely depends on whether one thinks of Jesus more as the elder brother to be emulated or as an authority through whom we learn to think rightly of God and neighbor. There is nothing about process thought to determine which of these emphases is more important. And the general openness of process thought suggests that both have their place.

God was in Jesus. Even a process thinker who is not a Christian must acknowledge that. Jesus' response to God has had world-historical importance for good and ill. Few would deny that.

---

[1]John B. Cobb, Jr., *Christ in a Pluralistic Age* (Philadelphia, Westminster Press, 1975).

Christians find grounds in their belief in Jesus' importance in the scheme of things to repent of the great ill that has been worked in his name. We are empowered by the field of force[2] he generated to seek ways to understand our world and to serve our neighbors wisely. We are inspired by what we learn from him to serve others even when it is costly. We are assured through him that God loves us and forgives us for our sins and failures.

Can process theology make sense of the creedal claim that Jesus is true God and true man?

The gospel of John says: "The Word became flesh and lived among us" (Jn. 1:14). This notion of incarnation is very congenial with process thought. Incarnation means that something is really and truly constitutively present in something else. However, although process theologians can feel some real enthusiasm for this doctrine, it has caused a great deal of trouble conceptually in the history of the church. And today, of course, it is still a bone of contention. It is a source of much hostility to Christianity, both within and without the church. Jews are offended by the doctrine of the incarnation; Muslims are offended by the doctrine of incarnation. But also among Christians are those who say, "This is nonsense. It is quite

---

[2]Cobb developed his idea of a "field of force" in *Christ in a Pluralistic Age*. There he writes that the reality of Jesus' life and death "has established a sphere of effectiveness or a field of force into which people can enter. To enter the field is to have the efficacy of the salvation event become causally determinative of increasing aspects of one's total life" (117). Cobb thus sees a threefold pattern of salvation. First, the words of Jesus become the occasion for Christ to be realized in the hearer; second, one enters his field of force; and third, through progressive conformation to him, the believer experiences "new being in Christ," or the creative transformation of the past into something novel that results in flourishing for the believer and enjoyment for God (see p. 125).

impossible for God to become a human being. That way of thinking is essentially mythological."

I agree. The doctrine of incarnation is often formulated in ways that seem to me to be mythological. But I also think there is a way of thinking about incarnation that is faithful to John's gospel and does not partake of that mythological and distorting character that others, including many Christians, rightly find offensive. Some have called the idea of a God Incarnate a false notion that Christians should now get rid of; I do not agree with this. I do not want to get rid of the notion of God Incarnate. I simply want to understand it in a way that is not mythological.

Myths tell of gods taking on different forms and becoming something other than gods. Think of Zeus taking the form of a bull. When he becomes a bull, he is no longer on Mount Olympus. Zeus is wherever the bull is, and, at least according to the story, the bull did not stay on Mount Olympus. This is not what the Christian doctrine of incarnation is about.

In the early church there was a tremendous struggle over an influential view that was similar to the story of Zeus's taking on another form. The view was that of Arius, and it was eventually declared a heresy, but the struggle lasted one hundred years. During that time, Arianism was sometimes the dominant Christian belief.

Arius believed that before God created anything else, God created a super-angelic being who was designated to be the savior of the world. This super-angelic being remained with God, and God also used this supreme creature as an instrument for creating all things. Now if you think in those terms—that a supreme creature was with God in heaven from before the foundation of the world—it is possible to think of such a being as taking on human form and becoming Jesus of Nazareth. That was Arius's theory.

However, when that supreme creature took on the form of Jesus, in the body of Jesus, that supreme creature was no longer in heaven. This is what actually happens when a being moves from heaven to earth, because once on earth, the being ceases to be in heaven. This is analogous to Zeus's taking on some human or animal form.

Many passages in the New Testament were interpreted to support Arius's view, but eventually the church decided against Arius on two counts. First, if you are an Arian, you do not believe that the divine reality you encounter in Jesus is truly God, and second, if you are an Arian, you do not believe that Jesus is truly human. Jesus is a metamorphosed form of a super-angelic creature, neither God nor human. The church struggled with these ideas and eventually formulated its final answer: Jesus is truly God and truly human.

Some people, unfortunately, have kept the idea of a metamorphosis and tried to apply it to Jesus, with some strange results. If you take it literally, during the period that Jesus was on earth, God was not in heaven. God was nowhere else, in fact, except in Jesus. No theologian ever went that far, but it is an implication of the belief. That God ceased to be God in order to be Jesus does not make sense, and it is an unfortunate understanding of the notion of incarnation that we would do well to eliminate.

But if that notion is untrue, what can we say about Jesus? Some people want to emphasize that the way God was present in Jesus is not fundamentally different from the way in which God is present in the believer. Some would say this is a matter of degree, that there is a perfection in the way God was present in Jesus that is lacking in others. We therefore look to Jesus as the revelation of what it fully means for God to be constitutively present.

The church, however, has wanted generally to emphasize a distinction between the way that God is present in Jesus and the way that God is present in the world in general. I do think this is right. God is incarnate in everything, not just in Jesus, but God is distinctively present in Jesus. The question, then, is how?

If we shift our thought from human substances to human experiences, it is possible to speak of God's being present and even constitutive of the very self. Let's unpack that. Within any experience is some kind of organizing center of that experience. I call that the "self" or the "I." How is it that "I" am constituted in any given moment? I think that the "I" as it ordinarily functions in my experience is constituted by a relationship to my own past experiences. Anything that comes to me from outside my own direct past experiences has the feel of being something other than me. In other words, there is a tension, or distinction, between the self and the other.

In principle, there is no reason that a human experience could not have its organizing center in the relationship to God, or the mode of divine presence. I cannot testify to this; I merely suggest that it is not an inconceivable notion that God might be incarnate, not simply as an "other" within experience but as its very center. In this case, self and other are experienced not as a tension but as a unity. Mystics have testified to this kind of unity with God. As I read the New Testament, despite the intimacy of Jesus with the one he calls "Abba," he does not seek or claim this mystical union. His personal identity through time remains strongly established. Accordingly, I suggest that the very self of Jesus was jointly constituted by the way he related to his own past (as you and I do) and by the presence of God within him. It is this unity in Jesus that is distinctive.

Incarnation in this sense reoccurs moment by moment, so that we can say there were times in Jesus' life when that experience of unity with God was broken. That is, when we come to the famous cry of Jesus on the cross, "My God, my God, why have you forsaken me?" we can take it seriously. When Jesus was in the wilderness, we can see that he really was tempted. These stories imply that Jesus' unity with God was not a metaphysical or physical given, but rather something that characterized his life and his experience by virtue of its being renewed moment by moment.

In this way, we can distinguish the full and radical incarnation of God in Jesus from the way in which God is incarnate in the world in general. We also have a way to speak of incarnation that is not mythological and that encompasses an idea of Jesus as "truly God and truly human."

In what ways can Whitehead's process philosophy help process theologians understand the doctrine of atonement?

Sometimes by atonement we mean any theory of the salvific work of Jesus. Sometimes we mean a rather specific theory, such as that of Saint Anselm, about how Jesus' death opened the way for God's forgiveness of our sins. In the former sense, all Christians must have some idea of atonement. In the latter sense, there are other options. As in so many instances, approaching the question of how Jesus is Savior from a process perspective does not in itself predetermine the answers. It does rule out a number of answers, and Anselm's, taken narrowly, is one of those. Although process thought affirms that there are changes in God's experience, it denies that God changes from unwillingness to forgive to willingness to do so as a result of a historical event. The particular way in which Anselm conceived the two natures of Jesus also seems incompatible with a process perspective.[3]

Before Anselm, the dominant theory was quite different. It located Jesus in the course of a cosmic struggle between God and Satan. In one of its versions, it depicted Satan as holding sway over the world and God as seeking a just way of breaking

---

[3]See *Cur Deas Homo,* in Anselm, *Basic Writings* (Chicago and LaSalle, Ill.: Open Court, 1962, 2001).

that hold. By cloaking the Son in human form, God deceived the devil into seizing and killing him, thus freeing God justly to break Satan's power over history.

The crudity of this story paved the way for its displacement by Anselm's. But in its broader form of God's struggle against the powers of evil in this world, it is quite congenial to a process rendering. Of course in process thought, God struggles to bring what good can emerge in every event whatsoever, and the results play some role in all future events. But process thought does not suppose that all events have equal weight—some obviously have vastly greater effects for good and evil than others. Christians thinking in process categories can reasonably assert that the Christ event is of all events, at least for them, the one that contributes the most to our good. Unpacking how it does so is one good way of discussing the "atonement."

The influence of the Christ event is present everywhere today, whether it is recognized or not, for the working of a past event in the present does not depend on consciousness. Among those who recognize it, it has power even when this is not appreciated or trusted. But it is where people have faith in Christ that the power for good is greatest. We Christians also renew and deepen our relation to the event through preaching and sacrament, thus strengthening its efficacy in our lives.

A major element in the influence of the Christ event is the way it opens us to the present working of the Holy Spirit. It shapes our understanding of God so that we can trust God. It reduces our defensiveness by making us willing and able to acknowledge the reality of who we are. It makes us aware of the importance of being receptive to God's empowering and directing presence. Thus it changes our relationship to God, not by changing God's attitude toward us but by opening us to gifts God has always wanted to give.

We can state this change in terms of the power of sin. We are all prone to be self-centered and defensive. We are also prone to give our loyalties to objects of limited worth and to develop hostility toward those who differ from us. Cumulatively these individual sinful characteristics generate "powers and principalities" that exercise enormous power in the world. We are largely shaped by these structures of society and by the ancient distortions they mediate to us.

This need not mean that we are all individually prone to physical violence, lying, or cruelty to the individuals with whom we deal. In such respects as these, some of us are, and others are not. But we are all members of communities whose collective behavior produces hideous exploitation of the poor throughout the world and in our own country renders many hopeless. We live in a racist society, which does not cease to be so because we individually disapprove. We could go on to tell of other principalities and powers to which we are bound.

Jesus was killed not so much by the individual sinfulness of particular people as by the principalities and powers of his time. But his life and death did, in some measure, break the control of those. His followers found that they could create communities that formed life in a different way, enabling them to distance themselves to some extent from the powers of evil in society. Even where outwardly they could be destroyed by those powers, inwardly they could maintain a measure of transcendence.

Of course the story is complex and ambiguous. The church established to free us from the control of evil often itself becomes oppressive and unjust. Christians, moved by the freedom they gain by faith in Christ, have sometimes had to act against the visible church and establish new communities to counter the principalities and powers. Nevertheless, it is possible to read history in terms of a victory "in principle" that we can continue to try to realize "in fact."

I have accented the cosmic struggle and its historical outcome. But this same account can lead to speaking of personal forgiveness of personal sin in the relationship with God made possible by Jesus and our relationship to him. The intensely

personal account more featured by Anselm is complementary
to the more historical one that I have emphasized.

If Jesus Christ is our Lord and Savior, who is Gautama Buddha?

For a long time Christians viewed religious traditions as
inherently competitive. This was true of alternative forms of
Christianity. If the Catholics were right, the Protestants were
wrong. If the magisterial Reformers were right, the Baptists
and Quakers were wrong. If the Calvinists were right, the
Lutherans were wrong. If the high Calvinists were right, the
Arminians were wrong. And so forth.

It took a long time for the denominational attitude to
replace this mutual exclusivism. Now most of us take for granted
that none of us has the exact and perfect form of Christianity
but that all of us have some contribution to make. What divides
us is not as important as what unites us as believers in Jesus
Christ. Institutional unity and theological agreement may not
be possible, or even desirable, but in some way, we do want to
express the unity of our faith before the world.

When we confront Buddhists, some adopt the older,
exclusivist attitude. If the Christians are right, the Buddhists
are wrong. Other Christians extend to Buddhists the
denominational attitude, believing that they constitute another
form of the same basic faith and commitment. Sometimes it is
proposed that there are many paths up the same mountain. We
follow Jesus up the mountain. Buddhists follow Gautama.

From a process perspective, this image is not very helpful.
We should allow others to define their purposes and goals
instead of assuming they are the same as ours. This can be a
problem even in the Christian ecumenical context, but there

we are dealing with other communities that do affirm with us that Jesus is Lord and Savior. This provides a very important agreement and commonality. Buddhists not only fail to share this conviction, they do not seek "salvation" as Christians define it. Instead, their goal is enlightenment. Sometimes they too affirm that there are many paths up the same mountain, but they understand the top of the mountain to be the kind of enlightenment attained by Gautama.

It is possible to argue, of course, that at some deep level what Buddhists mean by enlightenment and what Christians mean, or should mean, by salvation is the same. Some Christians are so impressed by Buddhism that they redefine salvation to conform to Buddhist ideas of enlightenment. But this is a high price to pay for mutual appreciation!

It seems much more honest to acknowledge real differences. Christian salvation and Buddhist enlightenment are not the same. Christian teaching guides us better in thinking about salvation. Buddhist teaching guides us better in thinking about enlightenment. They need not be contradictory or even competitive. It seems that to follow Jesus as Lord and Savior need not deter us from following Gautama as guide to enlightenment.

This possibility of adopting multiple religious traditions has been widely recognized and adopted in the East. Indeed, it has been all too easily accepted there, at least from a process perspective. The multiple religious traditions are simply allowed to lie there with little or no mutual criticism or interaction. From a Whiteheadian point of view, this misses the opportunity to turn differences into contrasts.

To take just one example, Christians have emphasized the responsible self. We have stressed the importance of free decisions made in conformity with the purposes of God. Buddhists, on the other hand, have taught a doctrine of "no-self" that seems, on the surface at least, to undermine the responsible self.

Trying to understand the Buddhist "no-self," Christians often point to our teachings of "selflessness." But this goes only part of the way. Selflessness is understood in the context of an ethic of love, where one serves the other without thought of the self. It does not really mean that there is no self to think about. The Buddhist doctrine is ontological; the Christian, ethical.

Process thought can understand the Buddhist teaching much better. The Buddhists mean that there is no substantial self. The self is a construct, not a given. They teach that when we recognize this and cease constructing a self, we are open to reality as it truly is. Process theologians agree that there is no substantial self. Hence, on the ontological side, we affirm the Buddhist doctrine. We see no loss to Christian faith in rejecting substantialist thinking. But we see a value in the construction of the responsible self, with all its complex consequences in Christian experience.

To say there is a value in constructing the responsible self in no way denies there is value in the realization of "no-self." These are different values. The two religious traditions are structured around this difference. The question is whether they can be enriched by each other or must simply lie side by side, unaffected by each other.

Approaching matters from a process perspective, I hope that the two traditions can contribute to each other, enriching both. I call this "mutual transformation." On the Christian side, much has already happened. Millennia ago Christians made a place for Neo-Platonic mysticism within Christianity, even though there is little or no such mysticism in the Bible. Although Buddhist enlightenment is different from Neo-Platonic mystical experience, I am confident that it can also be assimilated into Christian life. In the process, Christians will learn much, and we will transform other aspects of our tradition.

We must recognize, however, that to practice Buddhist meditation as a Christian does not accord enlightenment the ultimacy ascribed to it in Buddhist tradition. Even there it is often affirmed that the enlightened one, out of compassion, shares the fruit of enlightenment with others. For Christians the value of any spiritual discipline will finally be judged by its contribution to the divine commonwealth, that is, the world in which God's purposes are fulfilled. Because I believe that Buddhist meditation can contribute, I affirm it. But its attainment in itself cannot be the end of life.

3

The CHURCH *and* *the* BIBLE

Can a vital church in the future be continuous with the church of the past?

This is a tough question. My answer is yes, but the no answer must be taken very seriously at several levels.

At a simple level, we know that the music of the past does not speak to many younger people today. Musical tastes have always changed over time, but the pace of change is now radically accelerated. A service of worship that is comfortable to older people is a downer for most of the young. Hence the churches that are appealing to the young are often new types of churches quite discontinuous from our old-line congregations.

The question is, no doubt, intended at a much deeper, more theological level. The church has organized itself around a set of beliefs that are no longer convincing to many thoughtful people. Today its most visible forms are trying hard to retain values that no longer appeal to many of us, especially with respect to sexuality and abortion. Often the church seems to be the dead hand of the past. A vital Christianity, then, must express itself in quite new forms.

The question, further, is whether even "a vital Christianity" is what is wanted. Do we not need instead a new spirituality that draws on many traditions and moves into uncharted waters? Is not the label "Christianity" an impediment to such a move, an effort to restrict its freedom to respond to the new situation, an insistence on parochialism in a globalizing context?

Those of us who believe that the Christian churches now existing can have a promising future, that, indeed, they have a very important contribution to that future, do not find it easy to make our case in face of the evidence of what is actually happening. Nevertheless, we still try. I believe that process thought can help.

Jay McDaniel has written a book called *With Roots and Wings*.[1] Continuity with the past constitutes the roots. When these are strong and healthy, they free us to try our wings. Even a new spirituality, in fact, has roots, but when these are not acknowledged and celebrated, or when they are extremely eclectic, they may not make possible trying our wings. Sometimes the spirituality remains so individualistic that the strength we all draw from community is not garnered. Sometimes, in order to maintain community without affirming

---

[1]Jay McDaniel, *With Roots and Wings: Christianity in an Age of Ecology and Dialogue* (New York: Orbis Books, 1995).

a shared tradition, authoritarian methods are employed and a cult develops. There are, in other words, disadvantages in starting afresh.

Of course the danger of accenting continuity with tradition is also obvious. This can bind us to the past and put blinders on our eyes with respect to the present and future. We see many instances of this.

But many Christians find their roots in the tradition liberating and empowering. Much vitality exists in the church today among individuals and small groups who have found in the gospel a lever against oppression and exclusion and also against the dominant values of the consumer society. Other believers sometimes respond when these aspects of the tradition are brought to conscious attention. Whole communities within the church are shaped by this transforming vitality. In the midst of much decay and dreariness are seeds of new life.

Process theology can make a contribution to this development. In the process model, every momentary experience is both largely continuous with the past and in some measure new and different. The newness comes partly from drawing on elements in the past that were not there before. It comes most fundamentally from God, who enables us to weave these new elements together with the old through the realization of truly novel possibilities.

This microcosmic model speaks also to the macrocosmic Christian movement. When we trace its history, we see that it has always been in a process of change. When the change is healthy, the church is appropriating new wisdom from its environment, integrating it with its inherited understanding. Over centuries, it incorporated much of the best of the Hellenistic world. It also has incorporated much of the best of the Enlightenment. Yet there are always stresses and strains in this process. Not all its members accept change. Some identify rootage in the tradition with refusal to be open to the new. But history encourages us to think that when Christians trust

God, individually and collectively, they open themselves to the living Spirit.

In the past fifty years, the encounter with novel challenges has come at record speed. We have become aware of how anti-Judaism has been integral to our positive faith in Christ. We have repented. We have become aware that our views of Indian and Chinese religions have radically failed to appreciate their positive achievements and potential contributions to all humanity. We have repented and sought dialogue rather than an imperialistic relation. We have come to see the evil in our negative attitudes toward sexuality and in our patriarchal patterns. Again we have repented. We have recognized that our historic anthropocentric teaching blinded us to the destruction of our natural environment. Here too we have repented.

These claims call for clarification. The "we" certainly does not mean all Christians. Many still continue to be anti-Jewish, to promote imperialist relations to other religious communities, to regard sex as inherently dirty, to support the domination of women by men, and to encourage the exploitation of other creatures. Nevertheless, on each point, the change has been remarkable. Almost all Christian groups have changed on at least some of these points. Most of the old-line Protestant denominations have changed on all of them. For example, they are now struggling to overcome their deep-seated prejudice against those whose sexual preference is for persons of their own gender.

The second qualification is more serious. Our collective repentance has gone only halfway. Repentance includes regret and the effort to cease doing what we have been doing that is wrong. But it also means moving in a different direction. That requires widespread rethinking of the faith.

Too often it appears, even to ourselves, that our repentance is a compromise of our tradition. That by repenting we become less Christian and more something else, secular perhaps. We need instead to show how the deeper elements in our tradition enable us to criticize and reject the ones we now see as destructive. We need to show how we can learn from others, not by abandoning our own roots but precisely because of the nature of those roots.

We have not done this well. We have left the impression that in changing, we are cutting off many of our roots rather than sending our roots deeper. As a result, there seems to many to be less and less reason to think that Christianity has something of great importance to contribute.

Process theology can help. We can show that in the endless process of creative transformation that is called for, we are in fact following Christ. We can show that it is precisely our faith in God that leads us to draw on resources from outside our own tradition. We can show that faithfulness is expressed in risk-taking rather than in seeking security.

In those congregations that have faced all these challenges and moved forward, enthusiastically claiming their repentance as itself an expression of faith, we see a vitality that is our hope for the future. Whether that hope will be realized, we cannot know. Perhaps, in fact, the church will fail to seize its opportunity, will stop repentance halfway and continue in its present lukewarmness. Then we must expect that God will call into being new communities that are discontinuous with the past forms of the church. But we can hope that the church is instead passing through a new, and perhaps more difficult, reformation, and that there will be new life on the other side.

Is Christianity a cultural-linguistic system or a socio-historical movement?

Recent decades, have seen a great emphasis on language. We speak of the "linguistic turn" in philosophy. Some who stress the importance of language give the impression that reality consists in nothing else. Whitehead shared in the recognition of the importance of language. This is especially clear in *Modes of Thought,* where he writes that it is hard to say whether the human soul created language or language created the human soul.[2] Nevertheless, it is also clear in Whitehead that reality is not reduced to language. However important to our interpretation of reality language may be, there is a reality it is interpreting. And through physical feelings, we are in touch with that reality, albeit largely unconsciously. Whitehead's realism makes a huge difference. Of the many places this difference shows up, one is in the understanding of Christianity. A few years ago, George Lindbeck wrote a book called *The Nature of Doctrine,* in which he described Christianity as a cultural-linguistic system. The book has become something of a classic, and the idea of Christian faith as a cultural-linguistic system has become influential.[3]

Process theologians can agree with much in the book. Lindbeck criticizes two alternative views of the nature of doctrine. One is the propositional view that identifies Christian truth with a set of unalterable statements of belief. Process theologians certainly join in rejecting this view. The other is the experiential one, which teaches that there is an unalterable experience that gains expression in changing language. Against this, he rightly points out that our experience is already informed by language. We not only describe our experiences differently at different periods and in different languages, but experience itself changes. For help, Lindbeck turns to Clifford Geertz, a cultural anthropologist who has reflected on the relation of culture and language. It is Geertz who provides the idea of a cultural-linguistic system that at its depths remains constant even through many superficial changes. To be a part of a cultural group is to be formed by that linguistic system.

---

[2]Alfred North Whitehead, *Modes of Thought* (New York: Free Press, 1968), 40–41.
[3]George A. Lindbeck, *The Nature of Doctrine: Religion and Theology in a Postliberal Age* (Philadelphia: Westminster Press, 1984).

Lindbeck proposes that we think of Christianity in this way. If we do so, we see that the future of Christianity depends on socializing new generations into this linguistic system. This is quite different from teaching that a certain set of propositions is objectively true and that all should accept them. It is also quite different from cultivating a certain type of experience that can then be articulated in ways that make sense in changing contexts. From a process point of view it may be superior to either of those approaches.

Nevertheless, it is quite unsatisfactory in two major ways. First, it is essentially static. Although it recognizes surface changes, the "deep structure" of the symbolic system remains unchanged. From this point of view, what Christianity was, it is, and will be. The need is to socialize people into this system, not to reexamine it and hold up parts of what we have inherited for serious criticism and revision. Even if the Christian symbol system has been patriarchal, there is no basis for changing it into something else. If its implications are anti-Jewish, anti-Jewish they will remain. Greater efforts can be made to treat women more fairly and, certainly, to avoid persecution of Jews. The deep structure itself calls for justice and toleration. But it does not lead to more fundamental change.

Second, the cultural-linguistic system is self-contained. It does not refer to anything beyond itself—to God, for example. Every symbol has its meaning in its interrelations with the other symbols in the system, not by reference to something outside. This, in turn, has two problems. It makes interfaith dialogue impossible. Dialogue with persons who live in different linguistic systems requires at least the possibility of common referents of different symbols. These common referents may be either common objects or common experiences. If these do not exist, there can be no overlap of meanings.

This view rightly accents the difficulties of interfaith dialogue, the error of supposing that there will be simple correspondences of meanings between terms in the two systems.

But the actual success of dialogue demonstrates that differences among the traditions do not amount to sheer incommensurability. At a deep level, we do live in a common world, and some features of our experience of that world are similar.

Second, the denial of referents outside the system is in deep tension with the symbols themselves and the experience they evoke. The symbol *God* is not thought by believers to refer only to other symbols. It is believed to refer to that which existed long before there were any symbols at all and to transcend all symbols. The fact that *God,* like every word, is a symbol does not reduce God to a symbol.

The sociohistorical school out of which process theology arose had a better understanding. Christianity is a sociohistorical movement. Of course, symbols—linguistic and other— are very important to a movement. But they too have histories. They come into being and can also die. The death of any particular symbol need not be the death of the movement. A movement has many shared beliefs about the world in which it lives. As the movement reflects about these beliefs, the beliefs develop and change. Changes in the historical context also lead to changes in the belief system, so what seemed beyond all doubt in one generation may cease to seem credible in later times.

If symbols and beliefs change, what maintains the unity of the movement? The unity is more like that of a narrative or of a person's life. Tremendous changes occur, but there is no doubt that what is happening is a continuation of and development from what has happened before. Whitehead explained the unity of personal existence in terms of "hybrid feelings." In each moment, the most important prehension in my experience is usually of the antecedent moments of my experience. These prehensions include a great deal of conformation, so that in fact I am very much like what I was. But each moment has elements of novelty as well. The feeling of the novelties of one moment in the next moment, that is, physical feelings of conceptual feelings, are the hybrid feelings.

Hence, what I receive from my immediate past in one moment differs from what that past received from its past. This difference may be slight when compared with the massive similarity. But through hundreds, thousands, and hundreds of thousands of occasions, this difference can be very large. I am now the same "person" I was at the age of two, but my character and personality and the way I think are very different.

Not all changes are positive. Sometimes rich potentialities present at one point disappear because of the directions I choose. Sometimes I develop habits of rejecting anything that does not fit comfortably into what I have previously known. Sometimes I get in ruts and lose all memory of a richer and more complex past.

But most lives have many positive changes too. The most positive ones are those in which I am able to assimilate new ideas and sensibilities without abandoning what I have previously known and lived. This is not simply the addition of the new to the old, because assimilating the new also transforms the old. But transformation is not loss. We may think of the church in analogy to this. It is in continual change. This change may be decay, and change as such is not good. But there are healthy changes as well. When a sociohistorical movement is able to encounter others, learn from them, and move on enriched and transformed by that learning, it remains the same movement but stronger and wiser than before. Thus, a Christian movement that has assimilated scientific knowledge, historical knowledge, the wisdom of other religious traditions, and the perspective of women is a stronger and wiser Christianity than one that refuses all this.

Our old-line churches are in trouble today: their decline in membership and resources is a symptom of the decline in spirit. Lindbeck and those who follow him call for the church to emphasize its inherited language and separate itself from the influences of culture. But if the church is better conceived as a sociohistorical movement than as a cultural-linguistic system, this is the wrong recommendation. The church does need to renew its appreciative understanding of its own past, but it needs to do this so as to repent of its errors and sins and to wrestle with the challenges of the present. It is by nondefensively embracing truth and wisdom wherever they are to be found, not by holding fast to its old forms, that the church can be true to its own past and move confidently into the future.

Has process thought anything to contribute to the debate about homosexuality?

It is obvious that one cannot move directly from a metaphysical or cosmological model to a particular doctrine about sexuality. One of the weaknesses of process theology for some time was that it limited itself largely to questions about how God is related to the world because those followed most directly from its philosophical sources. But a theology must address the issues that disturb the church, and process theology must show how its understanding of God and the world bears on the questions about celebrating homosexual unions and ordaining homosexuals. Actually the connections are closer than one might think. This can be seen best by looking at the theological arguments against these acts. For the most part the arguments are based on three sources: scriptural texts, natural theology, and a doctrine of the created order. A process perspective engages all three and proposes a different way of dealing with the issues. Since the third is in some ways an amalgam of the first two, for the sake of brevity, I will address only those.

A process perspective emphasizes the importance of history and tradition. We are individually constituted by our life stories, and these are inseparable from larger, communal stories. To whatever extent we identify ourselves with Christians, the still larger story of Israel and the church are our stories. It is from these that we gain meaning and direction in our lives. Since later parts of the story look to earlier parts as their authority, and since the earlier parts are known through the scriptures they produced, these scriptures are of great importance to us.

Most of us are deeply grateful for the formative influences that have shaped our life stories. We celebrate what our parents and teachers and friends have done for us. But this does not mean that we affirm everything in our past. We have taken missteps, and sometimes others, those we trusted most, have led us astray. We repent of our mistakes and sins.

This must characterize our relation to our Hebrew and Christian past as well. We are deeply grateful for the values they have given us and for the great lives that inspire us. It is through our shared story that we know God. Even when we criticize our forebears in the faith, we do so from a point of view that they have bequeathed us.

Still, we must criticize. The Jewish scriptures tell the story of their heroes without concealing their failures and sins. That Christians have continued a history of failure and sin is overwhelmingly obvious. We must repent of much that we have collectively been. This includes biblical teachings, as, for example, the anti-Jewish teachings in the New Testament. Clearly the Bible is a thoroughly human document. That does not mean that it lacks inspiration. God was in those who wrote. But divine inspiration does not block out human historical conditioning or human prejudice. We can agree that insofar as homosexuality is discussed in the Bible, the attitude toward it is negative. But that does not determine that our attitude today should be negative. Whether that negative attitude is to be reaffirmed or rejected in terms of far more basic biblical teaching is to be decided anew in our time. The Catholic argument appeals chiefly to natural law, and Catholic thinking about natural law is based on a particular kind of teleology.

The idea is that sexuality exists for a particular purpose. Traditionally the church limited this purpose to procreation and taught that all sexual acts not oriented to procreation are sinful.

This doctrine has been softened in various ways, but the connection between sexual intercourse and procreation remains the basic natural law argument against sanctioning homosexual acts. The background, less acknowledged now than in earlier centuries, is that sexual activity requires some justification other than the enjoyment it provides. For process thought, enjoyment is a sufficient justification for activity—other things being equal. That is, every occasion aims at some enjoyment in itself and in other occasions lying in its future. Not only is there nothing wrong with that, that is the created order of things that we declare good. But of course that does not mean that other things are ever equal. Sexual acts aimed at immediate gratification while the participants ignore the likelihood of an unwanted pregnancy or of disease are not morally acceptable. Sexual acts unwanted by one of the partners are wrong. Sexual acts of adults with children or that exploit authority in other ways are to be rejected. Sexual acts that violate commitments made to others are immoral.

In addition to such strong negations of immoral sexual acts, Christians can rightly establish an ideal of how sexuality is best expressed. Most Christians judge that long-term, faithful pairing is important and that the ideal for sexual activity is that it occur in this context. That does not mean that all other sexual activity is to be judged always and everywhere wrong. But it does mean that a particular ordering of society for the encouragement of such partnerships is to be supported and that this ideal is to be celebrated.

The burden of proof is thus located by process theology on the opposite side from the dominant Christian tradition. Whereas the tradition stated that sexuality was evil and that sexual acts required moral justification, process theology asserts that sexual activity is good. What requires justification is the demand that it be restricted to particular channels. If we hold up one pattern of sexual life as ideal, we need to explain why and how this in the long run contributes to the greatest enjoyment of those who adopt it and of others who make up the society.

With this reversal, the need for special justification for homosexual acts disappears. They are to be affirmed except as there are reasons to restrict them. Christians generally, rightly in my opinion, believe that there are many good reasons to restrict them, just as there are good reasons to restrict heterosexual acts, and that the ideal for them, as for heterosexual acts, is that they occur within committed relationships. Through most of history it has been important to most societies to promote procreation, and most societies have pushed everyone toward marriage for this purpose. Some of them have been quite tolerant of homosexual activity as long as it supplemented, rather than replaced, procreation. We should not condemn our ancestors for seeking to channel sexual activity in these ways.

But today, in most of the world, the problem is too many people. The social reason for pushing people into heterosexual marriage no longer applies. There are still extremely important human reasons for encouraging such marriage for all who desire it, but there are good reasons to discourage those who are not sexually attracted to members of the opposite sex from entering such unions. For them, unions with others with whom the desire is mutual are far better.

Many heterosexuals decry homosexuals because of promiscuity. Surely the Christian response is not to condemn homosexuality, but to encourage more responsible expression. If heterosexual marriage were outlawed and heterosexuals were humiliated when they showed lasting attachments, one wonders whether the result would not be that heterosexual promiscuity would increase.

For these reasons, the process perspective leads quite directly to the judgment that the church should sanction and celebrate both homosexual and heterosexual unions. The issue of ordination is a more difficult step. Until the church sanctions, supports, and celebrates the union of sexually active homosexuals, ordination is awkward. But the proper response is not to pass strict rules against such ordination. The proper response is to sanction, support, and celebrate Christian union for active homosexuals.

A final word is in order. Process theologians know that the point of view that informs them, while far from limited to those who have studied process metaphysics, is still a break from the point of view that has been identified as Christian by the dominant tradition. We believe it is, in fact, more deeply faithful to the Bible, as well as to experience and reason. But we certainly understand how difficult it is for those formed, often unconsciously, by different philosophies and theologies to break with their implications.

Deeply entrenched is the notion of a Supreme Will who provides fixed moral laws applicable to all times and places and has revealed these laws once and for all in the Bible. This notion provides security and clarity in a sea of secular relativism. The clarity of our own convictions that this is not a mature Christian view should not be translated into the judgment that those Christians who hold it are less mature or faithful than we. We can instead have confidence that step-by-step the Holy Spirit will lead all who are open to that guidance to a fuller and more appropriate understanding. But meanwhile, we will act on the light that we have.

What role does the Bible have in process faith and theology?

Clearly a process thinker cannot affirm Bible inerrancy or literal historical accuracy. What, then, does it affirm? What does process thought say about the nature and authority of the Bible?

I believe I have dealt with this general topic before, but it is of such importance that I am happy to make another try. In doing so, it is important to recognize that the answer to this question depends not only on the influence of process philosophy on one's thinking but also on the Christian tradition that has shaped one. A Catholic will view this matter somewhat differently from a Calvinist, even if both are process theologians. I will give my own views as a Wesleyan process theologian.

For me, to be a Christian is to believe that the history of God with the Jewish people, culminating in Jesus, is of universal importance for humanity. This does not exclude the possibility that the history of the quest for enlightenment culminating in Buddha is also of universal importance. But to be a Christian is to stand in the tradition of Israel and to identify with the community that traces its self-understanding to ancient Israel through Jesus. For us the record of the history that has formed us spiritually is of extreme importance. The Christian Bible is the church's book, and the church is the continuation of the history of which we learn in the Bible. Without the centrality of the Bible, the church ceases to be the church.

It is in the context of this recognition of decisive importance that we ask the question of the nature and authority of the Bible. For process thought, there is a strong inclination to assert that inspiration has played a large role in the writing and formation of the Bible. But inspiration is not something supernatural. God works in all events; an element of inspiration is present in all creative thought. I believe a great deal more inspiration is manifest in the Jewish scriptures than in the chronicles of Mesopotamian kings that have been uncovered. But if we compare the scriptures with Plato, the contrast is far less apparent. The degree of inspiration, while important, is not the main issue with respect to authority.

God was active in the events that are reported and interpreted in the Bible. This is the view of biblical writers, and it is the view of process theologians. But again, God is active in all events whatsoever, so this does not distinguish

Jewish history from that of other people. The Bible itself makes this clear. But the Bible is unusual, if not unique, in its sustained interpretation of human events in relation to God's activity in the world. It invites us as no other literature does to understand the whole of human history in relation to God's purposes and actions.

As we follow the Bible's lead in this interpretation, we find much in the Bible with which we cannot fully agree. God is claimed to have authorized actions that are inconsistent with what we learn of God through the Hebrew prophets and through Jesus. God is said to have established laws that we believe are human, all too human. We have good reason to think that the events to which the Bible refers were not just as the Bible recounts them. Sometimes we sympathize with those the Bible vilifies. In faithfulness to the Bible, we criticize the Bible and argue with its authors.

Does this mean that we do not accept the Bible as authoritative? Far from it. If we rejected its authority, we would simply ignore it. It is because we affirm its authority that we argue with it. What is important is that as we argue with biblical authors, we recognize that the basis of our argument comes from the Bible and the tradition it has generated. For Christians, it is often from the point of view of the gospel accounts of the life and teaching of Jesus that we argue with authors of certain other biblical texts. But sometimes our criticism comes from what we have learned in more recent years from historians and scientists and is directed at the gospels as well. Then it is important to affirm that our learning from later thinkers and scholars is itself faithful to the biblical tradition, which is informed by the wisdom of Babylon, Egypt, and Greece.

From the point of view of fundamentalists, this under-standing of the nature and authority of the Bible may be shocking. It is also disturbing to secularists. Why, they ask, engage so intensively with one ancient body of literature? Why not turn away from that and find guidance and direction in contemporary natural and social sciences, along with philosophical ethics and the insights of great poets and novelists? Why work with a literature that is so full of error and archaic moral and religious ideas?

I have tried to answer that question in part by the way I opened this discussion. Whether it is better to understand ourselves in continuity with ancient Israel or to drop that connection and simply root ourselves in the modern and postmodern world is a fair and open question. Of course, what we call the modern world is in fact deeply rooted in ancient Israel, so the contrast is not so great. But for contemporaries, it is possible to appropriate the wisdom of the Enlightenment without looking further back. Why not seek the truth with the best methods honed in modern times, and with these alone?

This is one way of putting the question: Why be a Christian? Obviously process thinkers do not have to be Christian. Certainly we cannot appeal to the authority of the Bible as the reason to be Christian. Nevertheless, one can give reasons that are informed by process thought.

Modern thought in and of itself, that is, cut off from its deeper historical roots, moves away from judgments of value and moral norms. It finds these ultimately mysterious. The result has been to abandon, as a secular culture, all values and requirements other than profit-making in the market. Most people recognize that this is inadequate as a cultural norm.

Yet those within secular culture who affirm ethical principles, whether utilitarian or Kantian, are in fact ultimately indebted to the older religious history. Even so, principles of this kind, when abstracted from cultural contexts, lack efficacy. Self-criticism within modernity points to the fact that what really shapes moral values and concerns are traditions and communities that live from them—not abstract principles. Certainly Christianity is by no means the only such tradition and community, but it is the one that has been most important in shaping most of us in the West. To participate in the ongoing life of the Christian community is one way of contributing to the wider world.

Sadly, much of the way Christianity has informed our culture has been harmful. Christianity has contributed to making us a culturally arrogant, patriarchal, anti-sexual, ecologically insensitive people. In one respect or another, other traditions and communities seem to have teachings more suited to the real needs of our time. One healthy response is to join one of these communities. Another healthy response is to participate in the reformation, transformation, and renewal of the Christian tradition. This can be done best from within.

Of course the choice is never as objectifying as this sounds. One remains in the Christian community, or joins it, because of some deep resonance and appeal. One participates in it because Christ seems worthy of ultimate devotion. But all of that is also affected by one's judgment of how one's life and work in the particular community affects the world as a whole. God loves the world, and from a Christian point of view it is the well-being of the whole world, not of the church in abstraction from the world, that should be the major concern.

All this is to say that the authority one accords the Bible is a function of one's commitment to participating in and transmitting the Christian tradition. I am one who has felt called to that kind of life. For me, therefore, the Bible has enormous authority.

Is the Bible inspired?

As for so many questions asked of process theology, the answer is that it all depends on what the questioner means. If the question comes from one who thinks in very conservative categories, the answer must be an emphatic no! The words of the text were not dictated by God. Certainly the hand of the writer was not controlled by God. And even in the more modest sense proposed by some proponents of divine inspiration of scripture—that God protected the authors from error—the emphatic no remains. The Bible is full of errors of fact, of moral judgment, and of theological teaching.

But if the word *inspired* is being used as in ordinary language outside the conservative theological tradition, the situation is quite different. We say that someone's performance in a concert or in a play was inspired. We speak of poets as inspired. Even a preacher may be inspired. That is, people may be moved by the Spirit in extraordinary ways. They may be so totally caught up in what they are doing that they are not consciously controlling their actions. What results exceeds the best product of their ordinary voluntary acts. A writer may find that sometimes the words "just flow." A composer may feel that the music "comes to her." Inspiration in this sense is rare enough to be greatly prized, but it is common enough that many of us experience it to some extent. Indeed, it is not altogether discontinuous from quite ordinary experience.

Process thought affirms that at a very basic level, all life is inspired. That is, there is no life at all except as God's Spirit participates in constituting us. It is that participation of the Spirit that leads to our being, in each moment, something more than the deterministic outcome of the forces from the past that also play so large a role in shaping us. The times when we think of ourselves as inspired are those when this creative novelty contributed by God's Spirit plays a particularly strong and effective role and is less inhibited than usual by the other causal factors in our lives. So process theology affirms not only that the common use of the language of inspiration is meaningful but that the inspiration is truly the work of God.

When we think in this way, there is no reason to be skeptical of claims that many passages in the Bible are inspired. Indeed, it would be artificial to think that ancient Hebrew poets and prophets experienced inspiration less often than our contemporaries. The contrary is a reasonable guess. Our contemporaries are on the whole less intentionally open to God than were the Hebrews, and it is at least plausible to suggest that openness to God's inspiration is conducive to it. Also, the results that come down to us show many indications of inspiration.

The high ratio of inspired passages in the Bible is partly due to the process of selection, as no doubt there was much very ordinary writing in ancient Israel. What we now have was selected by the community through the centuries. That a community selects on the whole the more inspired parts of what is available is to be expected.

What follows from the judgment that much of the biblical writing is inspired in this sense? Certainly not that it is free from cultural influence or class bias or patriarchal perspective. The writings are thoroughly human, and that means just as conditioned as any writings by the contexts in which they arose. But to be conditioned is not to be wholly determined. It is in the element of transcendence over that determination that we find the work of the Spirit. And there is much of that creative transcendence in the Bible.

What follows from this judgment is that we do find God's truth transmitted to us in very earthen vessels. The texts we encounter deserve our deepest respect. Of course they should be studied by all critical methods, but when the assumptions of the critic are reductionistic, we must be open to more than the critic finds.

But is this to be said only of the Bible? Certainly not. There is inspiration in the writings of the ancient Greeks and Hindus and Chinese as well. There is inspiration also in the writings of Shakespeare and Goethe and of contemporary poets and dramatists. All this deserves our respect and listening.

Hence, the question of the uniqueness of the Bible cannot be answered by the category of inspiration—it must be answered in terms of the importance for us of the history of Israel. That history consists of events and their interpretations inextricably connected. Without inspired interpretations, the events would not be important to us today. But without unusual events, the inspired writers would not be more important than the inspired writers of other communities. For us, as Christians, the most important events are those that surrounded the person of Jesus. If it had not been for these events, the history that has shaped us would have been a very different one. These events would not have been possible apart from inspired interpretations of previous events. We cannot appropriate them today apart from interpretations, and if these are not inspired, our tradition will die. Thus, inspiration is involved at every point.

So my answer as a process theologian is that "Yes, the Bible contains much inspired material." The healthy continuance of our Christian tradition depends on our intense appreciation of that material and continual recurrence to it. It depends equally on our distinguishing inspiration from any notion of inerrancy. And finally, it depends on our inspired interpretations of that inspired material through relating it to all the wisdom we can gain from other sources.

Today we may be inspired to reject some of the ideas that are found even in the most inspired passages of scripture. We have been inspired to see through patriarchy, for example, a patriarchy that pervades the Bible. In this and other respects, we must preach against the Bible. But if this negation is to be healthy, it must be qualified in two respects. First, we should continue also to listen to the truth even in those passages that we feel have done most harm and continue to be most dangerous. And second, we should recognize that, at least for many of us, the call to attack biblical ideas is grounded in just that tradition we attack. For example, when we attack particular ideas of the prophets, our doing so continues the prophetic tradition. We may be taking the inspiration of the Bible most seriously when we are most free to critique its specific teachings.

How does process theology interpret the Bible? For example, if people can become demon possessed, why didn't God warn Moses about this when He warned him about sin in the Ten Commandments? Why did God sentence man to death and hell, but woman through childbirth is saved? If we have dominion over animals, why can they eat us? God is an image of light; so was Adam created in His image, or man's? Is the garden of Eden in heaven? Why does Jesus say if you cast out devils in his name, he will tell you to "depart you that work iniquity"? Didn't demons and devils originate in Babylon? Why did the Jews adopt the Babylonian Talmud? Have you seen the tabernacles on Mount Carmel that Daniel spoke of?

This set of questions arises from a way of reading the Bible that creates endless difficulties and confusions. It might be possible to deal with them one by one and give some kind of sensible answer, but that would not be very helpful. I will instead offer a few comments from a specifically process perspective, recognizing that most of what I say could be asserted by almost any Bible scholar in the old-line churches.

The Bible is a thoroughly human document written, edited, and compiled over many centuries by numerous people. From the perspective of process thought, to say that it is thoroughly human does not exclude God from involvement in its authorship. God is present and active in every moment of human experience, and in some moments God's activity, the Holy Spirit, is more effective than in others. In extreme cases we may properly speak of someone as inspired; there are many inspired passages in the Jewish and Christian scriptures.

But inspiration does not by any means entail inerrancy. An inspired author may rely on inaccurate historical information and prescientific notions of the natural world. Inspiration does not guarantee that a writer fully transcends the cultural values of the writer's time and write for all the ages. Hence, to press even the most inspired words in the Bible for accurate information or definitive judgments will often lead to absurdities.

Christians are fortunate that the Bible does not make the claim to be inerrant or even consistently inspired. In a few places individuals do make strong claims for what they have to say. For example, a prophet may assert that the Word of the Lord came to him and say, "Thus says the Lord." We should take these claims to extraordinary inspiration seriously. But we should also note that what follows are typically statements directed to particular people at particular times and places. It remains for us to discern their relevance today. Despite this lack of claim to divine inspiration in most of scripture, many Christians want to claim inerrancy and infallibility for every passage in it. This is a witness to the human tendency to idolatry—treating the earthen vessels as if they were God.

We are now heirs of two centuries of biblical scholarship based on assumptions of the sort I have sketched. Some of it is iconoclastic and largely negative. That type of scholarship has an important role in clearing away idolatrous attitudes toward the Bible.

Most biblical scholarship is extremely helpful in giving us access to the astonishing richness of insight and deep wisdom of the ancient Jews. This insight and wisdom had to do especially with the relationship of God and the world, and no other literature, ancient or modern, supersedes this in illuminating these most important of all questions. The Bible remains our basic source for reflecting on these matters.

For this purpose the diversity within the scriptures is very valuable. One cannot simply agree with everything one finds there. There are contradictions, and there are depictions of God in some of the earlier writings that a Christian simply cannot accept. But for the most part the diversity of experiences of God reflected in scripture enables the Bible to speak to us now in many and varied conditions and situations. Passages that one generation ignores often become crucially important to a later one.

Several of the issues posed by the questioner deal with the Genesis account of creation, stories that contain internal contradictions as well as prescientific ideas about how the world came into being. But when we recognize this and move to the deeper theological level, they are immensely important for good and ill.

For many generations, the stories were read as authorizing human exploitation of the natural world, but in the past few decades we have realized that this exploitation is threatening to render the Earth uninhabitable. This has brought us to repentance.

It has also brought us to study the creation stories afresh. We have recognized that although human beings are given a central place in the stories, all creatures are affirmed as of value, and the human role for which the stories call is not so much that of exploiter as of steward. The theological importance of these alternative ways of understanding the relation of God, humanity, and the other creatures is not affected by the recognition that the stories are told by fallible human beings and cannot be relied on for factual accuracy.

Of equal importance is what the stories say about the relation of males and females. Of the two creation stories, one sees male and female as together constituting the human that is created by God. The other definitely subordinates woman to man. It is this subordination that has dominated the history of Judaism, Christianity, and Islam. Today we must expose this account for the patriarchal prejudice that it expresses and establishes.

On what grounds can we pick and choose among biblical passages and themes?

This is the heart of the theological question today. For Christians, the answer is that we read all of the Bible from the perspective given us in Christ. But that is only the beginning of an answer. We must go on to clarify what we mean by Christ and how Christ is related to the historical Jesus. Are the words of Jesus our final authority? No, not if that means that they are treated literally and legalistically. But in the way Jesus points to God's love of us and our calling to love God and fellow creatures, we find a purity of inspiration that guides all our critical reflection about other ideas and themes in the scriptures.

It is sad indeed that for so many people being a Christian is associated with an idolatrous understanding of the Bible. The writings that should liberate us to think critically and creatively in ever new situations have been turned into bonds that tie us to ancient and outdated notions. We become absorbed in petty and even silly questions that have nothing to do with faith in Christ. Paul's distressed question to the Galatians applies to the contemporary church as well: "Having started with the Spirit, are you now ending with the flesh?" (3:3).

I have often been asked by fundamentalist Christians where the Bible explains God as changing. My response has been, "The whole Bible shows a changing God." This is not sufficient for those seeking a proof text. My premise and the fundamentalist premises are different, so I am not sure how to respond.

That the whole Bible shows a changing God is certainly the most important answer. It does so by taking time seriously, on the one side, and showing that God interacts with the creatures, on the other. What we do matters to God.

Nevertheless, the question of particular texts is a valid one, and there are many of them. Every time God is said to speak to someone or to appear to someone is a change, because God is not always speaking or acting in just that way.

If there is a problem, it is that these texts sometimes present such anthropomorphic depictions of God that process theologians are as eager as the tradition not to take them literally. For example, in Genesis 3:8, God is heard walking in the garden. Surely God does not always walk in the garden, so this is a change if we take the story literally. But even fundamentalists are likely to qualify this story in some way.

More important are the many texts in the *King James Version* that describe God as "repenting." We associate repenting so much with the confession of sin that these texts seem quite strange, and newer translations typically avoid the term. But repentance does not always entail acknowledgment of sin. It does require a change of direction or intention.

In the *King James Version* Genesis 6:6 reads, "It repented the LORD that he made man on the earth, and it grieved him at his heart." The *New Revised Standard Version* says, "And the LORD was sorry that he had made humankind on the earth, and it grieved him to his heart." Whatever translation one uses, this certainly depicts a change in God from the time when God, on completing the creation, saw that it was very good.

Exodus 32:14 is another example. In the *King James Version* it reads, "And the LORD repented of the evil which he thought to do unto his people." The *New Revised Standard Version* again avoids the word "repented" and simply reads, "And the LORD changed his mind about the disaster that he planned to bring on his people."

This passage is of particular interest because the change of mind is the result of Moses' pleading with God. Clearly there is interaction between God and human beings. God acts upon and within human beings; human beings address God; God is affected by what they have to say. Such interactions are not uncommon in the Jewish scriptures.

Another example is found in Amos 7. Here the *King James Version* twice states that God repented as a result of Amos' pleading that destruction not come on Israel. The *New Revised Standard Version* states that God "relented."

Of the dozens of other examples that could be cited, I select a longer passage from Psalms that speaks in quite typical ways of the interaction of God and God's people (Psalm 106: 43–45). The *King James Version* says: "Many times did he deliver them; but they provoked him with their counsel, and were brought low for their iniquity. Nevertheless he regarded their affliction, when he heard their cry: And he remembered for them his covenant, and repented according to the multitude of his mercies." The *New Revised Standard Version* reads, "Many times he delivered them, but they were rebellious in their purposes, and were brought low through their iniquity. Nevertheless he regarded their distress when he heard their cry. For their sake he remembered his covenant, and showed compassion according to the abundance of his steadfast love."

It is really rather surprising that fundamentalists should doubt that God changes. For example, many of them believe strongly in the efficacy of prayer, and the Jewish scriptures describe the efficacy of the prayers of Moses and Amos and of the cry of the people. They unabashedly state that God acted differently because of these prayers. Do fundamentalists wish to deny this with respect either to the biblical accounts or the present world?

Resistance on the part of fundamentalists to the idea that God changes comes from the tradition, not the Bible. The tradition was deeply affected by the Greek view that it is better not to be moved or influenced by anything external to oneself. The Stoic and Epicurean ideals were of men who were indifferent to what took place externally. Aristotle's God contemplated only Godself. If it is bad to be interacting with others, God must surely not do so! Thus the church reasoned officially. Christians could not change the Bible, so they interpreted it. The real truth, they declared, was that God was eternal, wholly beyond time and change, and unaffected by them. Time is real for us but not for God.

Fundamentalists in theory align themselves with the Bible rather than with Greek philosophy. But the power of the tradition is so great that they often resist acknowledging the difference. Once they have acknowledged it, in consistency they must attribute to God a good deal more changefulness than do process theologians!

For example, Moses is depicted as reminding God of things God has forgotten in the passage leading up to the Exodus quote above. The attribution to God of forgetfulness of the past cannot be taken straightforwardly by process theologians who share with the tradition the affirmation of God's omniscience. Also, the dramatic shifts from the intention to destroy a whole people to forgiveness based on a single conversation with one leader do not fit the process understanding of God's unfailing love.

Process theology emphasizes not only that God is genuinely responsive to what the creatures do but also that people have matured in their understanding of God. As the tradition recognized, much in the Bible cannot be taken as literal truth about God. Our criticism of the tradition is not that it recognized the need to question the literal factuality of biblical stories. It is that in the process of doing so, it substituted one understanding for another. For a biblical understanding of the interaction between God and creatures in a real history, it substituted the Greek notion of a timeless eternity. It replaced a God of loving vulnerability with a God who could not be affected by the suffering of the creatures or by their prayers.

For this reason the questioner is right to appeal to the Bible as a whole rather than to individual texts. The growth of Israel's thought was away from the crude anthropomorphism of some of the earlier writings, but it was not away from the conviction that God cares deeply for every creature and interacts with all creatures. The move of traditional philosophical theology away from that vision is the one that process theology protests.

What is the relation between process theology and openness theology?

Overall the relation is friendly, supportive, and overlapping. Of course there are differences and disagreements. I think the difference is primarily that of the context and constituency of the two theologies. The disagreements reflect those differences.

Openness theology is the outgrowth of the experience and reflection of thoughtful and sensitive members of the conservative evangelical community. They have seen that some of the doctrines that this community has inherited are not consonant with either Christian experience or the Bible, and they have undertaken to modify them. They do not see this modification as in any way contrary to evangelical faith, and it is important to them that the changes they are making are in no way a compromise with secular culture.

Process theology, on the other hand, has attracted some people who react strongly against conservative forms of Christianity. They are often people who have wondered, both for intellectual and existential reasons, whether they could believe in God at all. Some have reacted against the way the Bible has been imposed as an arbitrary external authority. Some trust philosophical reflection more than the theological tradition, and some are more interested in coherence with contemporary science than with orthodox theology.

What is remarkable is how close these two movements have come in the content of their affirmations. Both reject the impassive, nonrelational God of traditional philosophical theology. Both reject the idea that everything that happens is a direct expression of God's will. Both strongly affirm human freedom and responsibility. Both emphasize the goodness and graciousness of God, putting love central among God's attributes.

Openness theologians argue for these views scripturally, and process theologians do so philosophically. But this difference is far from total. Openness theologians are interested in the reasonableness of their beliefs, and Christian process theologians are interested in their faithfulness to the basic message of scripture. Since the lines are not sharply drawn, there are those who feel comfortable in both communities.

One doctrine on which a fairly clear line of disagreement can be drawn is divine power. Although the two groups largely agree on how that power actually operates in the world, it is important to those rooted in the evangelical community to affirm that God's giving us freedom and responsibility is a voluntary divine decision. God's power is such that God could control everything, but God chooses to limit the exercise of that power so as to make room for creaturely freedom.

Process theologians reject this solution on three grounds. One is the problem of evil. If God could have stopped the Holocaust and failed to do so in order to honor the freedom of the Nazis, we find God's judgment highly questionable. The second is the nature of divine power. We believe that divine power is not coercive power, but empowering, liberating, and persuasive power. The exercise of divine power enhances the power of the creatures. It does not remove it. The third is the nature of being as such. In our view, to be is to have power. God could not have created powerless creatures, because the idea of powerless creatures does not make sense. To create is to share power with creatures.

This is not the place to pursue the debate. Nor should this disagreement block friendly cooperation and mutual respect between the two groups. Indeed, there is no reason that Christians should not identify in at least a general way with both. We who are Christian process theologians and do care greatly about the relation of our affirmations to the Christian scriptures are particularly gratified by the development of openness theology. Whereas we have recognized that in our reading of the texts we could be accused of bias and even eisegesis, the very similar reading of the texts by openness theologians is reassuring. We can claim scriptural support for many of our views with greater confidence.[4]

---

[4]Editor's note: A book grew out of conferences held in Claremont with openness theologians. It is called *Searching for an Adequate God*. Notes Cobb: "Clark Pinnock did most of the work of putting these essays together and deserves 95 percent of the credit. To my embarrassment, by insisting on putting my name first among the editors, he has given the impression that I made a major contribution. But it is a fine book, and I am proud to b associated with it." See *Searching for an Adequate God*, ed. John B. Cobb, Jr., and Clark H. Pinnock (Grand Rapids, Mich.: W.B. Eerdmans, 2000).

4

HUMANITY

How does love work?

The experience of being loved by others, including God, goes far beyond simply believing that others love us. It is an actual experience of that love. From a process perspective, this is in fact part of our experience all the time. We are prehending others in a way that internalizes the feeling they are having— in ourselves. A child who does not feel parents and/or caretakers in this way is permanently injured. If we can imagine feeling this love from no one, we must imagine a devastated condition.

To be surrounded by people who hate you is a deeply destructive experience that one can surmount only if one still feels the love of others—ultimately, that of God.

Most of us take for granted a basic level of loving support from others. In the retirement community in which I live, we all enjoy all the time the diffuse love of one another. It adds greatly to the quality of our life together. There is a good deal of this in families and in congregations, except in the most dysfunctional cases.

The feelings of each of us enter into the feelings of the others. We are members one of another. In Whitehead's terminology, we prehend one another, and what we prehend are the feelings of others, including their subjective forms. The subjective forms are the emotions. When we feel these emotions as directed toward ourselves, their inclusion in our experience is intense and effective. Also, our emotions tend to conform to the emotions we prehend in others. When others love us, we are able to love ourselves. We are also able to love others.

But because the love of others in the community is normally diffuse and relatively constant, we tend not to notice it most of the time. We take for granted a certain level of happiness and enjoyment that this climate supports. Because we do not notice it, we do not always appreciate it.

In my community it happens again and again that when someone is ill or loses a spouse or experiences some other tragedy, the diffuse love takes on a sharp focus. Acts of kindness, expressions of concern, and intercessory prayer, all directed to that person, multiply. The person in question feels the love of the community in a new and dramatic way. This outpouring of loving thought does not bring the spouse back, but it does help greatly in the difficult transition to single life. If the problem is sickness, the outpouring often helps in the healing process.

Once one understands the power of love, one understands also the stupidity and evil of the many blocks we put in the way of its dominance in our feelings, its expression, and its reception. We understand more fully the high calling of our congregations as places of mutual love and caring and how that can increase their ability to minister to the world. We appreciate more deeply the importance of extending love to our "enemies," both for their sake and because limiting our love reduces our ability to receive it from others.

Whitehead's account of how we internalize one another's feelings allows us to understand all this. He also helps us to understand that we are not wholly formed in this way. We also make decisions about how to respond. Because we prehend God as well as creatures, we may not be totally destroyed by the lack of human love. We may even rise above the hostile context and forgive those who hate us and persecute us. But for the most part, our experience of the love of others and of the love of God go hand in hand. In the midst of the outpouring of the love of neighbors, we are opened to experiencing God's love as well. Our openness to God reinforces our openness to neighbors.

This can be stated in quite technical process ways. The prehension of the loving feelings of other human beings breaks through our defensiveness and self-protection. We are willing and able to be more trusting. God's call, the initial aim, in that context is far easier to experience as one of love to be heeded and followed. Embodying that aim more fully involves greater love of our neighbors and openness to their love of us.

In small ways, this is everyone's experience. It may be experienced dramatically, as when my community responds to one's loss. Of course, in its intensity it passes. But it can leave a residue of trust and joy and of the knowledge of the power of love.

Process theology sees God as experiencing and luring an evolving humankind toward a higher state, but scientific materialism sees no purpose in evolution. Can you explain how process theology deals with the idea and origin of sin and the apparent absence of any purpose in evolution?

This is an excellent question, especially in the aftermath of the attacks on the World Trade Center and the Pentagon. All of us agree that the killing of masses of people who have done nothing to deserve death is a terrible evil. Many go on to call the perpetration of this evil a sin. Although *sin* is a theological rather than a philosophical term, it is an appropriate term for process thinkers generally to use—and certainly for process theologians. Nevertheless, it should be used carefully.

In the New Testament, the Greek word translated as "sin" is *harmartia,* which means "missing the mark." Whitehead describes every occasion as having an initial aim, often missed in the final form of the subjective aim. This missing is more characteristic of complex occasions, such as moments of human experience, than elementary ones. Hence, the role of sin is primarily in human events, and even among those, more in those of adults than in those of children. We may judge that it has become greater as society has become more complicated and has shaped experience in more complex ways. The question suggests this.

Why do we so often miss the mark? In general terms, this is because every occasion of human experience is influenced not only by God's lure but by many other factors. Among these, one's personal past plays a large role. The divine lure is in the direction of taking more account of others, while the pressure of the past tends to concentrate attention on one's private future. The divine lure calls for a response, often in tension with established habits, that is best in the new situation. Established habits work against the needed change. Emotion is another important factor. When we are bullied or attacked, we feel anger. We have had a national experience of such anger recently. This is a natural and healthy feeling that may help us to deal with a situation, but it often expresses itself in actions that our own principles and beliefs do not support. Certainly it may blind us to the divine impulse within us.

There are other tensions. Our ideals are shaped by particular traditions. Our teachers and ministers, and especially our parents, instill these ideals in us. These ideals usually pull us beyond ourselves, but they frequently call us to devote ourselves to one tribe, one community, one religious tradition, and one nation, even at the expense of others. The divine call would expand our horizons still further, but social expectations and pressures work against a full response. Thus our sincere beliefs, often our religious beliefs, resist the call of God. We are persuaded by the ideals into which we have been socialized that we ought to act in ways that in fact, at a deeper level, are in tension with God's purposes for us.

Today it is especially important to recognize that much evil is done in obedience to sincerely held convictions. In all likelihood, this is the case with those who flew planes into the World Trade Towers. They genuinely believed that theirs was a virtuous action. A process theologian will be convinced that at a deep level, these persons also experienced a call to spare the lives of innocent people. But in their conscious experience, I suspect, this voice was drowned out by the assurance of their friends and associates that they were doing God's will.

This phenomenon of doing evil with a clear conscience in accordance with the highest ideals of the group whose opinions one respects is not a new one. Christian history is full of it, with the Crusades a commonly cited example. Those who killed witches and tortured heretics believed they were doing right, at least in some cases. Hundreds of millions of children over centuries were taught by conscientious adults to regard their sexual desires as dirty and sinful. Gays and lesbians still suffer at the hands of "righteous" Christians.

Religious traditions are by no means the only ones responsible for such horrors. Nationalism has caused millions of people to kill one another. A young man is expected to be prepared to give his life for his country in the process of trying to kill other young men who are giving their lives for their countries. All are celebrated for their heroism and virtue. No doubt many of these young men have felt some pull toward recognition of the humanity of those they were fighting, and thus some doubt about the virtue of killing them. But usually this has been drowned out by the demand for total devotion to one's own nation. Almost certainly, more evil has been done by persons who think they are doing good than by those who set out intentionally to do evil.

Of course, this does not mean that conventional morality is always at odds with God's purposes. Sometimes it embodies hard-won wisdom that helps children discern what is truly good. But the good is often the greatest enemy of the best. And intense commitment to the established good often blocks God's call to broader horizons and adventurous novelty. With these comments in mind, I'll go back to the question of the origins of sin. No doubt there has been some missing of the mark since life began, perhaps even before. But sin implies a kind of responsibility we do not impute to actions apart from the emergence of consciousness and even of self-consciousness. Primal peoples were no doubt aware of missing the mark, though the focus was more on the objective damaging of relations than on the subjective state of individual persons, which is the proper locus of sin.

The Bible associates the emergence of sin with the movement from a gathering society (the garden of Eden) to the domestication of plants and animals. There is little doubt that this domestication required a domestication of human beings also, which introduced new tensions into personal life. It created types of property for which there was competition, and therefore violent struggle, and it turned many human beings into property as well. Much of the evil in human relations began with this fateful change. Even so, these ancient ancestors thought more of objective evil than of subjective sin.

In the first century B.C.E., during what Karl Jaspers has taught us to call the axial period, individuals in a number of civilizations became fully aware of themselves in their subjectivity and inwardness. At this point, there was heightened awareness of the unsatisfactory nature of this internal condition and of personal behavior that was undesirable. In most cultures the explanation of this wrong behavior was ignorance. In Israel, on the other hand, the focus of attention on God's will led individuals to recognize that they often disobey when they could do otherwise. In this context the idea of sin became important. Once it arose, it could be read back into the behavior of those who had acted without this particular form of consciousness. It could also be increasingly subjectivized, so by the time of Jesus, the emphasis could fall on feelings and attitudes and desires, even when they were not acted on.

To a large extent, from a process point of view, the "mark" is broadening the horizons of concern—in biblical terms, loving more neighbors more nearly as one loves oneself. Missing the mark, therefore, has to do with keeping the circle of concern narrow. It would be going too far to say that if people always widened the circle, conflict and evil would be avoided. The greatest widening that is possible in most concrete situations would fall far short of the universal concern of God. It would still leave open the conflict of one group with others. Greater intensity of concern for one's own family and community is healthy and necessary, as well as dangerous and destructive. The ideal of a world in which we loved all neighbors as ourselves remains a very distant lure! The questioner suggests that the scientific view is that our task is to outgrow our primitive heritage. No doubt there is some truth to this. But it could be understood to mean that the process of civilization has made us less sinful. This is extremely doubtful. Our primitive heritage certainly limited horizons of concern—largely to the tribe and its immediate environment—and as time has gone on, the importance of extending concern more widely has greatly increased. Our heritage from our past may be one of the obstacles to doing so. But much that has developed in subsequent times has been designed to focus concern and loyalty on narrow goals. Even our religious communities are often guilty of this. And as noted above, civilization brought into being many of the destructive tensions that have heightened the problem of sin. It is better to focus on our society than on our genes as we seek to understand sin and reduce its power in the world.

Finally, though process theology has a definite and important place for sin as voluntary failure to fulfill the call of God, we need also to recognize that like so many concepts, an emphasis on sin can do, and has done, great harm. Much of the explanation of many objectively evil acts is to be found in social and personal circumstances over which the actor had no control. Quickly labeling the actor as "sinner" has led to forms of treatment that do not express the understanding and love to which we are called. This labeling may be a greater sin than the original act. When sin is identified with violation of God's will, and that will is understood to be embodied in a set of rules, the legalism that results can be very destructive indeed. We are encouraged to silence God's call instead of to develop sensitivity to it. Of course, most violation of the rules is not out of sensitivity to God's purposes, and much of it expresses sin as well as uncontrollable conditions. But no set of rules can be more than a very general indication of the typical nature of God's call, and many such sets include social prejudices that have nothing to do with that call. This has been especially true in the area of sexuality, but the problem is by no means limited to that. The New Testament tries to free us from this close association of sin with obedience to law, but unfortunately, Christians fall back into this legalism again and again.

What is the value of the human race, and should it be saved? Although human beings may be unique because of our advanced level of self-consciousness, does this uniqueness and all that it has wrought outweigh the right for less sentient beings to have a habitat and simply exist?

At one level, this question could be simply brushed aside as irrelevant. The human race will not intentionally wipe itself out for the sake of other species, and probably no one would seriously advocate doing so. But at a deeper level the question is very important. What is our justification for making our own survival and well-being as a species so central to all our acts and moral assertions? Does that justification stand up to criticism?

Furthermore, ideas being seriously discussed in "deep ecology" circles, if taken straightforwardly, could easily lead to the conclusion that the moral thing would be the decimation if not the obliteration of the human species. The fact that advocates of the ideas do not draw the extreme conclusions does not render the ideas innocuous. History shows that ideas that seem remote from practicality in one generation can be taken seriously in another.

One idea of deep ecologists is the equality of all species, a principle that is stated quite forcefully by a number of thinkers. Fortunately, none of them today draws practical conclusions from that principle alone. For example, some introduce the idea that every species rightly places its own interests first. But there are tensions between their qualifications and much else that they say. Suppose that in another generation some people took the principle at face value and drew ethical conclusions from it. The question to which this essay is an answer would arise quite forcefully. If the well-being of the human species is no more important in the grand scheme of things than that of a species of beetle somewhere in the Amazon, and if the human species is responsible for the extinction of many species every year, surely doing what we can to eliminate or at least greatly reduce the human population becomes our moral responsibility.

Realistically it is very unlikely that the conclusion would be applied to those who adopt the principle. But it could greatly affect acts of the privileged and powerful toward others. If the privileged and powerful are convinced that the human population should be reduced, this will reduce their willingness to make sacrifices for the sake of the survival of starving people in other parts of the world. Writing off certain peoples or countries, as proposed by lifeboat ethics, will come to seem moral.

The "land ethic" can also be formulated so as to lead to a similar result. Normally this ethic is directed precisely to human beings to guide our relation to the land, calling on us to do what is needed for the health of the land. But if our very presence in the land is what causes its deterioration, the removal of that presence may appear to be the most moral response.

Process theologians share the conviction of the importance of biodiversity and the health of the land. But we do not formulate our basic principles in ways that could lead to the results noted above. We seek the greatest possible value in the whole scheme of things, ultimately as the whole exists in the life of God. We believe that all creatures individually contribute to the value of the whole, but that some contribute more than others. Of course our ability to rank creatures in this respect is limited, but our conviction is that the experience of a dog is much richer than that of a flea. We believe it is not merely human prejudice, but also objective fact, that the experience of a healthy human being is richer than that of the dog. We believe that if the well-being of the human species requires some loss of other species, such a loss can be sadly accepted as part of the tragic character of existence. For example, we do not greatly grieve over the eradication of certain bacteria whose chief function has been to cause human sickness and death. On the other hand, we do not deny that even those bacteria had intrinsic value, and their disappearance also involved some loss. And when the question is about beetles and birds and mammals, the loss of value from their extermination is far greater.

A second principle is equally important to us. This is that diversity contributes to value. An experience is rich to the extent that it holds diversities in contrast, and what makes human experience richer than that of the dog is that it is capable of holding more diversities in contrast. An important part of the diversity that enriches human experience is biodiversity. Hence, even for the sake of human value, the maintenance of biodiversity is important. The total value of other creatures is not just the addition of the value of each individual creature.

This is supplemented by the contribution of the diversity to the richness of experience of other creatures, and especially of human beings. This means that on the whole, the well-being of humanity and the well-being of other species are mutually supportive. For our own sake, we need to adopt the land ethic and act with a view to maintaining biodiversity. Deeply appreciating the intrinsic value of other creatures and their claim on us helps us to check our tendency to define our human goods in narrowly economic terms. When we allow the latter to dominate, as at present, we sacrifice not only other creatures but also our own long-term and inclusive good to short-term gains for the rich. Our failure to oppose this now-dominant policy is our greatest collective sin against ourselves, against other species, and against God.

Introducing God into our considerations undergirds the principles already given but also enlarges their application. One could argue from what has been said above that the loss of many species is unimportant. If one species is replaced by the expansion of another, so that the number of creatures of approximately equal individual value remains the same, and if the present number of such species far exceeds human imagination and appreciation, there seems to be no reason to deplore this simplification of the biosphere. That is, if the loss of a species does not reduce the total value of individuals, and if it has at most a trivial effect on the richness of human or any other creature's experience, it would be unimportant according to these principles.

For process theology, however, there is One for whom the whole diversity does contribute to richness of experience. That One is God. The contrasts available to God's experience are reduced whenever one type of experience ceases to be. In comparison with what it could be, God's life is impoverished.

The emphasis on the value of diversity in process theology gives strong reasons for opposing human expansion at the expense of other species. It also heightens the distinctive importance of the human species. Of course there is diversity within the experiences of members of other species, but the diversity among human beings far exceeds that within any other species. One reason that in the human case we place so strong an emphasis on the distinctive value of each individual is that individuals differ so much from one another. Those differences contribute to the richness of experience of each human being. They contribute also to God. If we compare a world without human beings in which a larger number of species lived well with a world with human beings, the loss of diversity would be enormous. Even if the latter world had moderately less biodiversity than the former, the total diversity would be greater. Process theology provides strong undergirding to a concern for human survival and flourishing.

The real questions for us have to do with proposing and supporting policies that will truly undergird human flourishing precisely by supporting the flourishing of other species. Such policies must deal not only with overcoming the primacy of economic measures but also with the human population. Global population is already too large for universal human flourishing in a world in which other species also flourish. We must seek policies that stop population growth and eventually reduce human population, but which do not themselves undercut the human dignity so essential to present flourishing. Excellent proposals worthy of our support have been offered, at a 1994 UN conference in Cairo, for example. They do not go far enough, but even they are not being implemented.[1]

A major obstacle to adopting these policies and, even more, to considering more drastic ones is religious-philosophical. In the dominant Western traditions, the value of individual human life has been absolutized. The above paragraphs make clear that for process theology individual human life is of great value, but it is not absolute. Only if it is de-absolutized can the Cairo policies be adopted and additional steps be taken. The potential value of the fetus is great, but it must be weighed against other values in a context in which overpopulation is a serious problem. Similarly, it is important that elderly persons be treated with great respect, but such respect does not entail denying them the right to a dignified death when life ceases to be a positive value for them. Allowing people to move freely across national boundaries is an excellent ideal, but when it prevents the adoption of population policies that are crucial for a

---

[1]For information about this conference, see http://www.iisd.ca/linkages/cairo.html.

desirable future, it must be restricted. These are hard choices, but the truth in the concerns underlying the question indicate that they are important ones. If we do not make hard choices now, we will be forced to make truly horrible ones later.

Can you comment on the tension between faith and direct religious experience?

Much Protestant theology focuses on what we believe. The left wing of the Reformation included some who emphasized personal, immediate experience of the divine, but the major Reformers did not. This highly personal experience was often appealed to as providing authoritative information, and the Reformers were rightly suspicious of such claims.

Of course they did emphasize experience. The belief that God has saved us in Jesus Christ deeply affects experience. If one has feared that God is angry with one because one has sinned, belief in God's forgiveness comes as a great relief. But this shaping of experience by belief is quite different from the shaping of belief by experience.

The primacy of faith did not exclude direct experience of God, a point that was made in some streams in the Anglican tradition and most effectively by John Wesley. These elements in Protestantism continued the experiential focus of some of the left wing of the Reformation, maintaining space within Protestantism for some forms of mysticism.

In the early nineteenth century, Schleiermacher proposed a more radical move to the primacy of experience. At the height of the Romantic Movement, he recognized that asking people to believe in the authority of the Bible was not effective. Unless they could understand Christian faith as growing out of actual, personal experience of God, it would not be meaningful to them. Schleiermacher taught that the deepest level of religious experience was the feeling of being absolutely dependent, which was, in his view, the experience of God. Schleiermacher's theology played an important role in liberal Protestantism.

In the twentieth century, however, this appeal to immediate experience has been sharply criticized. Neoorthodoxy emphatically returned to the primacy of faith over experience. In philosophical circles, there has been extensive criticism of the idea that there is experience of any kind that is not culturally conditioned. This is true *a fortiori* of religious experience. The emphasis has been especially on the primacy of language, and this emphasis can be used by Protestant theologians to reinforce the primacy of faith as faith in the word.

Ironically, just at the time that intellectuals reject experience as a source of knowledge, and especially of religious knowledge, widespread interest in spirituality has arisen in the culture. "Spirituality" means many things, but one element within this interest is immediate, personal experience. Some are not interested in the experience of God, but even among these, those who believe in God in the process tradition may discern that they are speaking of God. The God they have rejected is often the God process theologians have also rejected.

To say this, of course, is to presuppose that, unlike most Protestant theology, process theology affirms the direct, personal experience of God. Indeed, process theologians believe that we prehend, or feel, God in every moment. We know that this is rarely conscious, and we know that conscious experience of God is always also affected and interpreted through culturally shaped ideas and expectations. But we are open to reports of conscious experience of God nevertheless. Some claimed experience seems to us confirmatory of belief that is also based on intellectual arguments and more general phenomenological considerations.

Is there a process spirituality?

If we were to select one form of traditional Christian spirituality that is most clearly encouraged by process thought, it would probably be the spirituality of discernment as practiced by Jesuits and Quakers. Whitehead tells us that in every moment, we are being directed, called, or lured by God to that self-actualization that is best for that moment and also for future occasions in our own personal life and in the lives of other creatures, human and nonhuman. We can embody that fresh possibility for our lives more or less fully, and the more or less may make a huge difference to ourselves and to others. Clearly it is important to discern what God is calling us to be and do, to distinguish this lure from the many other impulses and urges that function in our experience.

A special strength of Jesuits and Quakers, from a process perspective, is that they emphasize both deep individual interiority and the community. The call comes to each one individually, moment by moment. No one can tell us what that call is. Nevertheless, our capacities for confusion and self-deception are great. Accordingly, especially when the call is for unconventional behavior, it is important to talk with others about it. Some may be able to discern that we are mistaken and help us to see that this is so.

What we need, of course, is to develop a habit of openness to God and readiness to respond even when this is somewhat costly in relation to our other appetites and desires. The special practices of spirituality may help us develop such an attitude. This is the chief function of spirituality.

Although discernment is obviously important, process thought has many other implications for spiritual practice. One interesting direction to explore is in relation to Buddhism. The process model of "the many become one and are increased by one" is very close to the Buddhist understanding of "dependent origination." Both lead to the rejection of the idea of substances underlying the phenomena. Events or processes are primary. Because Buddhists have developed meditational practices over the millennia that follow from this understanding, it would be presumptuous for us latecomers to develop our own without first learning from them.

Buddhists have found that freeing themselves from the view that they are self-enduring selves brings release from many of the problems of life. Process thought also denies the existence of an underlying, substantial self. Following Buddhist practices can contribute to spiritual growth for process thinkers, and Buddhist disciplines also help to liberate practitioners from imposing concepts and emotions generated in the past on what is given in the present. The disciplines encourage, instead, attention to just what is as it is. This is also a fruitful type of spiritual discipline from a process perspective.

One emphasis of process thought is on the distinction and integration of "soma" and "psyche." Western thought has often reduced the psyche to mind, but for process thought, it retains much else. Whitehead used the Western translation of psyche, that is, "soul." But for many in the West, that concept has religious connotations that confuse the discussion. Hence, I will use the richer Greek words. Many forms of spiritual discipline neglect the soma or even emphasize its subordination. These are uncongenial to process thought. On the other hand, spiritual disciplines have demonstrated that psychic states have a great effect on the condition of the soma. Spiritual healing both of one's own body and of others is a reality. This makes sense from a process perspective, since there is every reason to engage in spiritual practices that make for a healthy body. Process thought cautions, on the other hand, against going too far. Some theories of spirituality have denied the body autonomy or even reality. Process thought insists on the reality, importance, and partial independence of what happens in the body. A few spiritual disciplines encourage awareness of the soma and appreciation for it, and these are certainly appropriate to process spirituality. The more fully disciplines recognize the integration of soma and psyche the better. Process thought objects only if the great importance of the soma for the psyche is exaggerated in such a way that the distinctness and partial independence of the psyche is obscured or denied.

It would be possible to identify other forms of spirituality that are supported and affirmed by process thought, but I want to conclude by drawing some implications. The implication is not to identify one form of spiritual discipline to be practiced by all who adopt process thought; it is more to show how these can be regarded as complementary to one another. Different people may need different practices. The same person may need different practices at different stages of life. More fundamentally, I suggest from a process perspective that some people may have no need for special disciplines. As Christians we are free to engage in distinct spiritual practices, but we are not bound to do so. We are to be disciples, and if special practices help us to be better disciples, they should be encouraged. For most people, this is the case.

If we think of prayer and worship as spiritual practices, we may need to modify the emphasis of the preceding paragraph. If we understand prayer broadly as a way of bringing our relation to God to awareness, it is hard to imagine a Christian life that does not include it. If we understand worship as doing this as a community, out of our belief in the importance of community, Christians in general, and process Christians in particular, will normally and normatively involve themselves in worship.

But the forms of prayer and the forms of corporate worship can vary greatly. Like the Sabbath, prayer and worship are made for human beings, not human beings for them. Perhaps the most important spiritual practice for the process Christian is that of Christian freedom.

What meaning does prayer have for process theology?

Most traditional forms of prayer make good sense from a process point of view, much better sense than from the point of view of classical philosophical theology. But it may be important to make a couple of negative points before beginning the positive. Some popular beliefs about prayer have destructive consequences.

First, the effects of events about which one is praying are much the same as the effects of other events. We should not suppose that the fact that we are praying makes those events discontinuous from others.

Second, prayer is not a form of magic. It becomes one factor along with many others in determining what happens. It does not displace the others. Everything we do makes a difference to us, to the world, and to God. One of those things we do is pray.

A prayer of thanksgiving and praise is unproblematic. We have much to thank and praise God for. To feel grateful is healthy and appropriate. To express it benefits all.

Prayers of confession are fully understandable. They can be occasions for honest self-examination when we have failed to do and be what we could and should have done and been. They can contribute greatly to self-knowledge and have a positive effect on future motivation and behavior.

Such prayers can also have ambiguous effects. Sometimes people judge themselves by impossible standards and their prayers intensify feelings of unrealistic guilt. In relation to these standards, no real change may be possible, so the same sin is confessed again and again. Something may be gained from this emphasis on our individual participation in the sinful condition of humanity, but something is lost if the result is intensification of feelings of helplessness and dependence. The repentance that is to follow confession is a real change of direction, rather than a wallowing in collective human guilt. Of course, intensification of gratitude for God's loving acceptance of all humanity despite its idolatries can be a healthy change, but even this can distract attention from the practically needed changes toward which realistic self-examination before God can lead.

The main issue, however, concerns petitionary prayer. Does such prayer make sense in process theology? I think it does, but of course, it makes a great deal of difference what we ask for. If we pray for something that is contrary to God's purposes, for some harm to come to another, for example, that will make a difference. Our negative attitude may damage the other person; certainly it will damage us, and it will affect God as well. If we pray for something that is in harmony with God's purposes, such as a purer heart that will open us to allowing God's grace to act more fully and effectively in our lives, that, too, will make a difference.

A case of special interest is praying for healing. There is little doubt that praying for our own healing can help if it is done with confidence that God is already at work in our bodies in a healing way. We learn more and more about the effects of our mental and emotional states on the events in our bodies. Praying for healing is one way of aligning ourselves with the healing work of God.

Many of our prayers are for the healing of others. Can these prayers help? Here too, I believe the evidence is positive, and process categories can help us understand how. We are all prehending other people all the time. Their feelings and attitudes make a difference to us, mostly unconsciously. If they are directing their positive thoughts about us to God, this can certainly make a difference.

Obviously there are often ways of helping others that are more effective than praying for them. Giving them food and medicine and visiting with them are typically more helpful. In the New Testament, the tests are whether we have fed the hungry and clothed the naked, not whether we have prayed for them. If prayer is used as an excuse for not helping in other ways, we are not being faithful. But that does not deny that prayer can help too.

What process theology points to most centrally as the function of prayer is to open ourselves to God's gracious working in our lives and to seek to align our own intentions with God's call to us. This should be the total stance of our lives, not limited to times of prayer. But surely prayer can be an occasion for focusing on this relationship and overcoming obstacles to it. As we live more in harmony with God's purposes, we will act or pray as we are led, believing that what we do matters to others and to God as well as to ourselves.

But we will never suppose that what we do supersedes all the other forces that impinge on each event. Praying for recovery from a disease does not ensure that we will not die. Praying for a pure heart does not eradicate sin. Prayer is one factor among many influencing what happens—and it is sometimes a very important factor.

What are your views on immortality?

Christians have varied ideas about "immortality" and tend to cover up their differences with vague rhetoric. Behind that rhetoric, I encounter three general views with lots of diversity within them.

Some reject any notion of a reality other than our actual experience here and now between birth and death. They think that affirming anything of that sort is religiously damaging, because it encourages dualistic and otherworldly thinking. They believe that it has disparaged and distorted the real values of life here and now. They also believe that there is no valid reason to suppose that any other reality exists. If there is any "immortality," it lies in the reabsorption of our bodies into the ongoing processes of nature and in the influence of our lives, however slight, upon the future.

Some believe that the Christian faith holds out the promise that in the "end" all that has been still is, in some fulfilled or perfected way. Tillich, Barth, and Pannenberg all seem to assert something like this. This belief is required to undergird the meaningfulness of our otherwise utterly transient existence, individually and historically.

Others hold to the belief in continuing life after death, either immediately or after the end of history. To them, simply preserving what has been is quite unsatisfactory. Christian hope is for new life, a fulfilled and transformed life.

Process theologians can be found in all three camps. What may be thought of as "standard" process theology falls in the second one. This is Whitehead's Consequent Nature of God, and is the emphatic position of Charles Hartshorne.[2] Of course, process theology has the distinctive note that each occasion of human experience is retained in God (along with nonhuman occasions) and that this immortality is immediate. Marjorie Suchocki has developed this notion in such a way that it incorporates many of the values of the third camp as well.[3]

Although Whitehead's emphasis falls in this second camp, he also recognizes that his metaphysics allows for the continuing existence of primarily mental occasions after the death of the

---

[2]See Charles Hartshorne, *Omnipotence and Other Theological Mistakes* (Albany, N.Y.: State University of New York Press, 1984).

[3]See Marjorie Suchocki, *The End of Evil: Process Eschatology in Historical Context* (Albany, N.Y.: State University of New York Press, 1988).

body. This is unusual in the history of philosophy, because most metaphysical systems have either demonstrated the necessary truth of personal immortality or shown its impossibility. In *Religion in the Making,* Whitehead states that continuation of the life of the soul is a question to be settled empirically rather than metaphysically.[4] Some process theologians believe that empirical evidence is favorable to this belief.

The question is also one of judgment as to the religious value of such beliefs. It is rare that those who do not see religious value in the hope for new life after physical death judge the evidence favorable or even examine it with much interest. Hence, the judgments of positive value and of factual likelihood tend to go together, though some would like to believe in such life but think that to do so would be wishful thinking.

I count myself among those who think that belief in life after death can function positively today. I say this despite the extensive harm that it has done in the past, especially when salvation and damnation were defined in terms of such postmortem existence. Today the danger to a proper valuation of human life here and now seems to arise more from the tendency to view people as simply what they appear to be, in terms of their social functions, or even worse, reductionistically, as what they are seen to be in the physical sciences. The doctrine of the soul, which once functioned to disparage the body, may now be needed to preserve even the body from trivialization.

Because I think there is need for an understanding of the soul that indicates its partial transcendence of the body as scientifically understood, I am interested in the evidence for this transcendence, including that of the soul's continuation beyond physical death. But my attention to this matter has been sporadic. Anyone who is seriously concerned should read David Griffin. He has an excellent chapter on this topic in

---

[4]Alfred North Whitehead, *Religion in the Making* (New York: Fordham University Press, 1996), 110–11.

God and Religion in the Postmodern World.[5] As that chapter shows, there is a close connection among process thinkers between interest in parapsychological phenomena generally and concern about life after death. The phenomena, if they occur, indicate a partial transcendence of the soul in relation to the physical body. It is this partial transcendence that makes the idea of the soul's life apart from the present physical body conceivable. Griffin has written an entire book on parapsychology, the most thorough philosophical study of this topic in this generation.[6] Strictly speaking, the soul's survival of death need not amount to immortality. Indeed, for process thought, the notion of any form of creaturely existence enduring forever seems inherently implausible. The only immortality would seem to be in God, as both Whitehead and Hartshorne have emphasized.

My own way of speculating about these matters is to stress that personal identity is far from complete even in this life. Also, the Christian ideal is that we love others as we love ourselves. Really to do that would mean that our concern in each moment was for the whole future that we could influence, not focused on our personal future. One who has attained to that state will not be concerned about personal continuity beyond death. But others are, and God may give us that continuity as long we need or want it, but it will not be forever.

One feature of Whitehead's conceptuality is highlighted in discussion of this topic. It accents empirical inquiry and the diversity of faith perspectives. On most questions, therefore, it leaves open a variety of answers. Those of us who adopt his views still have to work out our own beliefs. But those beliefs will nevertheless be deeply affected by the fact that we view reality in terms of process.

---

[5]David Ray Griffin, *God and Religion in the Postmodern World* (Albany. N.Y.: State University of New York Press, 1989).

[6]David Ray Griffin, *Parapsychology, Philosophy and Spirituality: A Postmodern Exploration* (Albany, N.Y: State University of New York Press, 1997).

Can you elaborate on the process view of life after physical death? Are our satisfactions resurrected into God, and do they grow into what they could be in God's aim? Will we be able then to grow into God's aim?

This is more specific than the general topic of life after death. It is about the Consequent Nature of God and what it means that we are taken up into this. And there is no single answer of process theologians to these questions. There are slight differences between Whitehead and Hartshorne, and those who follow them also have different views. Of course, no one knows.

But even if we can only have visions of what may be rather than of what certainly is, these visions are important. To be persuasive, the visions should be organically related to the rest of what we believe. If they are to function eschatologically, they must at some level satisfy our need to believe that life and history have meaning, that they add up in some way, that what we are and do are not simply lost forever, and that even when a life is painful or seemingly vacuous, it makes some positive contribution.

This is the main point of both Whitehead and Hartshorne. Whitehead thinks it is more coherent to suppose that God has physical feelings of the world than that God only mediates pure possibilities to the world. He also thinks this belief makes contact with some very deep religious intuitions. For if God prehends us, there are good reasons to think that God's Consequent Nature includes us far more fully and richly than even a successor moment of our own experience includes its predecessors.

There are two dimensions to this difference. First, in every prehension of my immediate past experience, some of it is omitted. Whitehead provides good reason to think that in God's prehension, nothing, or virtually nothing, is omitted. Second, though the immediate past is felt in human experience with considerable immediacy, that is, its subjectivity functions as such, this fades rapidly. My memories of what occurred even a few minutes ago lack that immediacy. In God, there is no fading of immediacy. Each experience in its full subjective value lives on forever.

Students of Whitehead sometimes miss this emphasis on experiential immediacy in the divine life because this is said to be a doctrine of "objective" immortality. This is set over against "subjective" immortality, which means that persons would continue to enjoy new experiences after death.

This distinction is real and important, and though process thought does not exclude the possibility of subjective immortality in this sense, that is not what this question is about. The point here is that the data of God's physical feelings are our subjective experiences. It is these that live on in God in their full immediacy.

The question, however, asks for something more than this, something at which Whitehead hints. As occasions of experience are resurrected in the divine life, are they changed and do they continue to change? Specifically, do they grow into what they could be in God's aim? Marjorie Suchocki has gone further than any other process theologian in exploring this possibility. Her book *The End of Evil* is to be highly recommended for its speculative development of Whitehead's hints in this direction.[7] Her development of Whitehead's thought is motivated by her passionate conviction that sheer, everlasting perpetuation of miserable experiences is no eschatology!

---

[7]Suchocki, *End of Evil*.

I have not been able to imagine as much transformation within the divine life as Suchocki does. Nevertheless, it is clear that there is some. A creaturely occasion as felt by God is not simply what that occasion was as an act of creaturely feeling. Whereas it felt itself in a very limited context, it is felt by God in a universal context. In that context, it has a meaning and role that it did not have for itself. Further, as the Consequent Nature includes more and more events lying in the future of the one in question, the meaning of the original event changes. Since God's lures have taken account of the original event, the later events, when responsive to those lures, may have built in positive ways upon it. Thus, as time goes on, the momentary experience in question may become part of the realization of aims of which it was itself unaware, even of aims that did not exist at that time.

The question remains whether this change of role and meaning affects the subjectivity of the occasion. Here my imagination breaks down, and I am disposed to answer negatively. The subjective experience prehended by God remains forever just that experience. An experience here and now may be positively affected by the assurance that God can use it beyond its merits in the larger scheme of things. But just what that use may be lies forever outside the experience.

The added element of assurance that God will do with us more than we can imagine is important. That it probably does not affect the immediacy of our lives in God need not detract from that current value. It can provide the deeper meaning required by eschatological faith.

5

ETHICS *and* SOCIETY

Does process thought have a distinctive ethical slant?

That's a good question, and not an easy one to answer. Like so many good questions, it calls for an answer that says both yes and no. Process thought suggests a distinctive approach to ethical issues, but it does not clearly support any one of the standard ethical theories over against the others. I'll try to unpack this a bit.

Process thought discourages abstracting one sphere of life and thought from the rest. Therefore, it cuts against treating ethics as an independent discipline, separable from aesthetics and science and religion and metaphysics. Of course, it equally opposes treating any of these others in separation from ethics. On the other hand, there is no objection to starting reflection with questions about how we should respond to the issues posed by life. On the contrary, for many of us, this is the best place to begin. But we should not expect to get much help in answering these questions by turning to textbooks on philosophical ethics.

For example, in such textbooks one will find discussions of deontological and teleological ethics. The distinction is real and at a certain level has some importance. But process thought sees that elements of both are inevitably present in the decision-making process. Often the really difficult questions have more to do with the facts and how we interpret them than with theories about how ethical questions are answered.

Process thought implies that we *ought* to consider the wider consequences of our actions. That is, there is a deontological ground for adopting a teleological stance. The more difficult issue is how to evaluate anticipated consequences. Here process thought does contribute distinctive (not necessarily unique) elements to the discussion. I can note just a few:

1. Consequences are judged in terms of an understanding of value that emphasizes aesthetic qualities. See part 4 of Whitehead's *Adventures of Ideas* for the fullest elaboration.[1]

2. Animal experience counts in the evaluation.

3. There are gradations of value among the typical experiences of different species. We judge the experience of a whale as more valuable than that of squid.

4. Variety contributes to value.

5. All the values in the world add up in God and are supplemented by contrasts among these values in the divine experience.

---

[1]Alfred North Whitehead, *Adventures of Ideas* (New York: Free Press, 1967).

For a process thinker moral rules have a place in guiding our actions. They represent accumulated wisdom gained in experience. On the other hand, when moral rules are absolutized, they are likely to do as much harm as good. For a process thinker, generalizations are very important. We could not think or act without them. But it is equally important to recognize that in every moment, each person is located in a unique position never occupied before. Generalizations must be qualified in light of this. Process thinkers have long recognized that the position from which thinking occurs is historically and culturally conditioned. In recent years, we have learned more deeply that it is also conditioned by ethnicity and gender as well as one's place in the social hierarchy. On the other hand, process thinkers believe that in the midst of all this relativity, the possibility of some limited transcendence toward objectivity exists. The recognition of relativity is itself an expression of such objectivity exists. These comments are far from exhaustive. They may, however, help to explain why it is so difficult to write "a process ethics," though it is not difficult to write from a process point of view on critical ethical issues. That kind of writing exists in abundance.

It seems to me that process ethics would affirm the Buddhist precept about "no harm" unless absolutely necessary. On the subject of harming animals, does this mean God wants all compound individuals (and other entities capable of "high-grade" prehensions) to become vegetarians?

Buddhism teaches compassion toward all sentient beings. This constant refrain about sentient beings rather than just human beings certainly has practical and religious consequences. This is largely in continuity with Hindu teaching and has its greatest impact in South Asian cultures related to Indian culture. It has had less effect in China, Korea, and Japan, where Buddhism often seems hardly less anthropocentric than Christianity.

Process ethics, when not too distorted by its context in the anthropocentric West, definitely shares the view that we should have concern for the suffering of all sentient beings. Many of those most influenced by process thought, like many Buddhists, reflect this concern by being vegetarian. Others distinguish between killing for food and causing unnecessary suffering. Process thought is more clearly against the latter than the former. But since so much suffering is inflicted today in the meat industry, vegetarianism remains for these, also, a form of protest and refusal that should be supported.

The lack of unqualified support for not killing is related to the question, Does God want carnivores to cease killing herbivores? The answer, I think, is that if the actual course of events reflects in any way God's purposes, this is not the case. God seeks "intensity" in the world rather than anaesthesia, or the total lack of suffering. Strictly speaking, the goal of ending suffering for all sentient creatures would mean the end of sentient creatures. But God seems to have lured creation in a direction in which both suffering and enjoyment have been heightened. Clearly the God who shares the feelings of all sentient beings wants enjoyment to outweigh suffering, and probably, in the wild, this characterizes the lives of most sentient beings, even though these lives may be cut off at an early point.

If we examine how higher intensities of experience have come to be, we see that the predator-prey relation has played a major role. It leads to greater intelligence on the part of both, along with greater sensitivity. Herbivores whose development is not checked by carnivores seem to deteriorate as a species. Human hunting tends in the same direction, since humans seek the prime members of a species to kill, whereas carnivores go after the weak, the sick, and the old.

What does this mean for human action? I have indicated that I do not draw the lesson that all killing of animals is wrong. When the number of cats or dogs exceeds the number that can be cared for by humans, the Humane Society does us a service by killing them with as little suffering as possible.

The Humane Society rightly urges that we reduce animals' birth rate rather than bring them to life only to kill them. If farmers raise chickens and cows and hogs, and if they are treated well so that they can enjoy their lives, killing them for food seems to me in line with the general order of things and not to be forbidden. A mixed farming of vegetables and animals enables a farmer to maintain the ecology of the farm better than a monoculture of grain. When the Heifer Project introduces rabbits or goats into impoverished communities in the Third World, knowing that in due course they will be killed for food, the gain seems to me to greatly outweigh the losses. Once we have killed off all the predators of deer, hunters must take over the task of keeping the number of deer down, or the deer will suffer more keenly from starvation than from a bullet.

But when we return to the present reality, process ethics has as its primary role to protest the enormous suffering inflicted on domestic animals. We do not have a healthy farm ecology composed of livestock and plants. We have factory farming with monocultures of plants on the one hand, animals on the other, and destructive consequences to the land as well as to the animals involved. From the perspective of process thought, this is a profound distortion of the desirable human relation to other species and their individual members.

E Pluribus Unum?

For many years, this slogan was applied in the United States with an emphasis on the *unum*. We considered ourselves the great melting pot in which many—predominantly European—cultures were merged into the unified culture of the United States. Distinctive of this culture were its democracy and its use of the English language, and the public schools implemented these goals. Overall this program was remarkably successful.

Of course the program had its limits. The Roman Catholic Church recognized correctly that the public schools, as well as the culture they nourished, were Protestant in character. The church responded by creating its own system of schools. Nevertheless, in those schools as well, children were taught to speak English and to be good citizens of a democratic nation. Jews recognized the dominant American culture to be Christian, and, without opposing the universality of English or the democratic commitments, they refused to be fully assimilated. These religio-cultural differences caused many frictions, but they did not prevent American society from achieving sufficient unity for its needs. The more severe problem was with Native Americans, many of whom did not want to be assimilated at all. Christian missionaries worked with the government in schemes of forcible assimilation. For example, children were taken from their parents and educated in schools where they were punished for speaking their own languages or otherwise acting in terms of their own culture. The results were far from ideal. Nevertheless many, including even some Native Americans, saw no other future for these conquered people. The one group that was excluded from the goal of assimilation were African Americans, who were deemed to be inferior, and even after slavery was ended, most were educated in segregated and markedly inferior schools. In the South, they were legally segregated for their entire lives and excluded from participation in democratic processes. The civil rights struggle that ended legal segregation was fought in the name of integration into the dominant society. But before it ended, this ideal was strongly challenged. Why should a nation composed of many peoples require all of them to adopt an Americanized version of Anglo-Saxon Protestant culture?

Once this question was vigorously raised, people from many cultural backgrounds began to answer that this model of unity was unacceptable. The pendulum swung to the accent on "pluribus." It became "politically correct" to affirm that all citizens of the United States should identify themselves in hyphenated ways or compound ways. There are Italian Americans and Norwegian Americans as well as Chinese Americans. Of course, there are African Americans and English Americans as well. The breakdown into cultural groups can go further and further. Mexican Americans are quite different from Cuban Americans, and within Mexico are various regions. Then there are the Hispanics who lived in the Southwest long before the Europeans came. Now instead of concealing and denying features of their heritage that are in tension with the dominant Anglo-American one, people proudly affirm their distinctiveness.

In process perspective, how do we view this shift? We celebrate it. The process model of "the many become one" emphasizes that the nature and richness of the one is a function of the diversity of the many. The more the diverse contributions of the many can be retained in contrasts and contrasts of contrasts, the greater the value realized in the one. Negation of the differences, characteristic of the assimilationist model, impoverishes the one.

On the other hand, for process thought it is important that the many do become one. The one that is achieved will not be determined in its character by just one of the many that become it. It will be influenced by all. But it must have a unity of its own, a unity enriched by all. The many can retain something of their own integrity in this unity, but it must be an integrity that takes account of the rightful claims of other groups as well as the need of unity for all.

This process model is not easy to realize. It is in tension both with those who emphasize continuity with the older integrationist model and those who complain of any pressure on them to modify their inherited cultures. Because the new problems center on the ideal of cultural pluralism, I will focus on these. I will take public education as the key locus for reflecting about these problems.

A primary function of education has always been the transmission of adult culture to youth. Cultural pluralism cuts against doing this in schools. The schools can teach about the many cultures, but that is a very different matter. They cannot transmit the particular values of any one. Youth culture, with its emphases on instant gratification and peer acceptance, cannot be checked by strong affirmation of adult values. The values that are most obviously common to all are economic. Hence multicultural schools in fact function primarily in the service of the economy. Values that are subordinated in all the traditions now dominate over traditional values. Understandably many parents are dissatisfied and prefer to teach their children at home or place them in private schools. Many blame schools and teachers for this unsatisfactory situation, but there is little these can do. More money by itself will not resolve the problem. Unless the many cultural traditions interact with one another, enrich one another, and move toward a new form of unity that replaces the Anglo-American Protestant one with a richer unity, our problems will only grow worse.

The Whiteheadian model of the many becoming one is very similar to the American model of *E Pluribus Unum*. Its contribution can be that Whitehead worked out in detail how this unification of the many is best achieved. Process thought here points the way ahead on a critical and urgent issue. The work has been pioneered by Henry Young in his book *Hope in Process*, but there is much left to be done.[2]

Does process theology have anything to say about patriotism?

We are surrounded by a great resurgence of patriotism. My neighbors, for example, have had a flag out ever since September 11. Knowing them, I do not doubt that it expresses a healthy love of our country. But there are good reasons for Christians to worry that patriotism passes too easily and too commonly into a religious nationalism that is unacceptable. There seems to be a lot of that around. Does the process perspective throw any helpful light on this?

Process theology has two implications that at first blush seem to be in considerable tension. On the one hand, it strongly encourages us to view the world as we believe God views it. From that perspective, all creatures are important, and among them, human beings are especially important. Human beings in one culture or nation are not more important than those in other cultures and nations. Further, all are interconnected. It is the whole that should command our loyalty and concern.

From this point of view, we could view nations as necessary evils that should in time be superseded by global unification and government. We could argue that caring more for the people in one nation than for those in others is a violation of our deeper duty. If we reason in this way, it seems that patriotism is misdirected loyalty, a form of idolatry.

---

[2]Henry Young, *Hope in Process: A Theology of Social Pluralism* (Minneapolis: Fortress Press, 1990).

The second implication cuts in a different direction. Although we are in relation with all other creatures, the relations with our nearer neighbors are of far greater importance than those with remote creatures. Our responsibilities are correlative with this importance. That is, we can make a much greater difference in the lives of those who are most closely related to us than in the lives of those who are remote. If we tried to care equally for all children, our own children would suffer terribly. If everyone cared equally for all children, all children would suffer terribly. Viewing matters from this perspective, special love of our own country makes sense as an extension of special love for those with whom we are most closely connected.

For process theology, it is important to hold both sets of implications. Furthermore, it is not enough to hold them in tension with each other. We aim at coherent thought. We need a vision of the world under God that does justice to both sets of implications. And that is not as difficult as it may seem.

Whitehead sees the world as made up of individual occasions of experience. Some of these have no stable patterns of relations, and these make up empty space. The creatures in which we take primary interest are organized into societies. The organs of the human body, such as hearts, kidneys, livers, and brains, are societies, and the primary character and role of the member occasions are shaped by participation in the society. When some cells cease to participate positively in the societies of which they are members, cancer may occur. The health and well-being of the organs contribute to that of the body as a whole and depend on the health and well-being of the body as a whole.

The relations among people have important analogies to those among the organs in a single body. As the human body is a society of societies, so also human families can be thought of as societies of societies of societies, and larger groupings of human beings as societies of societies of societies of societies— and so forth. A nation is one of these more inclusive societies. The whole of creation is a much more inclusive society of societies. When any subsociety acts without regard for the well-being of the larger society of which it is a member, the result is analogous to that of cancer in the human body.

Of course, the analogy has limits. One limitation is that human beings have capacities that individual cells do not. We can be aware not only of the most immediate societies to which we belong but of the larger societies of societies as well. It is possible for children to be indoctrinated to subordinate their loyalty to family to that for the nation. Jesus called for a loyalty to his movement that subordinated loyalty to family. A globalist may ask us to subordinate all loyalties lesser than that to the whole. Human capacities for transcendence make possible such top-down patterns, and no doubt there are times and places where they are needed.

From the perspective of process theology, however, the subordination of loyalty to the more intimate society to the more inclusive one is not normally desirable. The whole is normally better served by healthy subsocieties. A nation in which parents fear that their children will betray them out of loyalty to the nation is not healthy. When family relations are broken by the conversion of individual members to a new religious community, much of value is lost.

On the other hand, if members of a family forget that the family is a member of larger societies, both the larger society and the family suffer. The deeper well-being of a family depends on being part of a flourishing larger society. It is in the long-term interest of the family to contribute positively to that larger society even at the expense of its short-term desires. Hence, each member of the family should seek to shape the family both for its own immediate well-being and so as to contribute to the wider society. Before September 11, the problem in the United States seemed more an indifference to the well-being of the nation as a whole than excessive concern about it.

The wider society exists at many levels and takes many forms. For the past several centuries the most important of these forms has been the nation-state. Because of its real importance, it deserves special loyalty from the individual persons and the societies that make it up. On the other hand the concentration of power and loyalty at the level of the nation-state has had many negative consequences. The state has often demanded that "patriotism" both supersede loyalties to the many societies of which it is composed and block loyalty to any larger society. When it does that, process theology must protest. The nation is but one society of societies and a member of a larger society. It has greater claim on the loyalty of those who live within it than does any other nation. But it deserves that superior loyalty only as it participates responsibly in the larger family of nations.

When the nation fails to participate responsibly in the larger family, especially when it acts in ways that are deeply harmful to others and to the larger whole, love of nation requires efforts to change its behavior and, as a minimum, to protest. True patriotism will say that "I love my country right or wrong." It does not say that I will obey the national leadership "right or wrong." When one believes that one's national policies are irresponsible and destructive, true patriotism expresses itself in calling for repentance for one's nation's sins and doing what one can to direct the nation's activity in the right channels. For those who believe in God, such patriotism calls for reminding the nation that God cares equally for other peoples and respects their love of their nations.

My own view is that the right direction today is to surrender some of the powers that have been concentrated at the national level to local communities and others to international bodies, such as the United Nations and the World Court. But the real danger currently is that we surrender national power to transnational corporations and the global institutions that encourage the dominance of corporations, such as the World Trade Organization. Hence, in the whole complex process of finding the right checks and balances, I find myself supporting patriotism as a provisional check on transferring power from political to economic actors. I also find myself allied with nationalists in their opposition to economic globalism. On the other hand, I oppose nationalists when they seem to believe that we have the right to inflict unlimited suffering on others if that preserves our own national security. In doing all this, I believe I am being patriotic, that is, expressing my love for country, in a way that process theology encourages.

Does process theology call us to be pacifists or to support just war theory?

Process theology does not lend itself to absolutes, whereas much pacifism proceeds from the absolute rejection of killing people. Hence, the answer might be a fairly simple no. But some forms of pacifism do not depend on absolutes. Pacifists can argue that war always does more harm than good, that there can be no solution to the escalation of evil and suffering by that means, and that we should, accordingly, envision and witness to other possibilities. This kind of argument a process theologian must take very seriously.

Marjorie Suchocki wrote a book redefining sin as unnecessary violence.[3] Part of her point is that sin is to be seen first and foremost as the evil we inflict on other creatures. Since war is organized and institutionalized violence of the most horrific sort, her argument certainly raises the question of whether war is ever "necessary."

That question moves us closer to the traditional just war theory. The church has tried to specify the circumstances under

---

[3]Marjorie Suchocki, *The Fall to Violence: Original Sin in Relational Theology* (New York: Continuum, 1994).

which it is morally right to go to war. The theory is good, but the sad fact is that the church rarely addresses controversial concrete cases well. Time after time only pacifists oppose unjust wars.

The theory requires not only that the cause be just but that in conducting such a war, the costs will be low. That is, even a just cause does not warrant paying a disproportionate price in the lives of one's own citizens. Neither does it warrant inflicting vast suffering on the people of another country. And the war cannot be deemed "just" if success in rather short order is not probable.

It is obvious that such a theory cannot support both sides in a war. If one is just, the other is not. Most often, neither side is justified. Yet rarely have churches condemned their own governments for going to war. It is true that at a late stage in the Vietnam conflict the Catholic bishops in the United States declared that it was not a just war. Unfortunately they did not seriously attempt to persuade American Catholics to oppose the war. This does not mean that there have been no just wars. It does mean that they have been rare and that the just war teaching of the church has not led to much opposition to the numerous unjust wars. In retrospect, we must acknowledge that pacifists have usually been right in their refusal to participate.

World War II is a good test case. There have been few instances when a nation has been led by a more vicious ideology in its effort to conquer others. Was the United States right to enter that war and thereby tilt the scales toward victory by the Allies? Surely this was a far better outcome than victory by Nazi Germany! Was the advantage worth the enormous destruction of life and property involved in attaining this victory?

I do not know the answer. Let us suppose that if we had not entered the war, Germany would have extended its rule over all of Europe. If there were no further resistance, that rule probably would not have been as harsh as wartime occupation policies, but the resulting Europe is not one we can contemplate happily.

On the other hand, the worst result of the extension of German power, the annihilation of the Jewish population of Europe, was not prevented by the war. We could have done much more to reduce Jewish suffering by speaking out strongly and admitting an unlimited number of Jewish refugees to our country than we did by fighting. If Great Britain would have been occupied, we could have evacuated Jews (and others most likely to have been singled out for genocide or punishment) from there beforehand. The cost of measures of this sort would have been tiny in comparison with the war.

But perhaps the Nazis would not have been satisfied to rule all of Europe. If we did not resist militarily, perhaps they would have conquered North America as well. Where then would the Jews have gone for refuge? How terrible would life have been under the global power of Hitler? How long would it have taken for German rule to have mellowed?

Or consider another pacifist scenario. For Nazis to rule other nations, they required the active cooperation of citizens, often leaders, in those countries. What if instead of military resistance, whole peoples practiced nonviolent noncooperation? The conquerors would then have to provide complete bureaucracies out of their own ranks. These would still find the work extremely difficult without the cooperation of ordinary citizens. Governing conquered nations would prove extremely costly and have few rewards for the conqueror. Of course the cost of nonviolent noncooperation would have been high. Perhaps tens of thousands would have been executed, but in comparison with the slaughter of war, it would have remained small. There are those who are convinced that if we devoted the resources we now put into military preparedness into preparing the nation for nonviolent noncooperation, we could deter conquest without the huge mutual destruction of war.

For Christians to decide that they are called to envision and witness alternatives to war, even when the enemy's victory is a truly horrible prospect, seems both reasonable and admirable from the point of view of process theology. Without such envisioning and witnessing, the prospect of the world reordering itself on a more peaceful basis is poor. Without severe critics of war the likelihood is that the churches in all countries will continue to countenance unjust wars. Pacifists have an important role.

The question of whether the Allied cause in World War II was just remains unanswered by all this, because the real options did not include systematic passive resistance. At the time, I judged the war just. To this day, I lean in that direction.

More relevant today is whether the war against the government of Afghanistan was just. A case can certainly be made for this. It was a winnable war in a short period of time. The government that was destroyed was unjust to many of its citizens, especially women, and it was hospitable to terrorists who had attacked us. There is a chance of replacing it with a stable, representative government that will be much more just to its people.

But a case can also be made against it. Our ostensible purpose, bringing to justice the chief suspect in the terrorist attack on the World Trade Center and the Pentagon, had a good chance of success through negotiations, which we refused. Our bombing caused many civilian deaths, and unexploded bombs are likely to kill more over the years. Far more deaths may be caused by the war's interruption of famine relief. Almost certainly the number of deaths resulting from the war will exceed all the deaths caused by all terrorist attacks to date and in the foreseeable future. There is no assurance that the new government will, over the years, bring peace and justice to Afghanistan.

Less relevant to the decision is the question of the relation of our real purposes to our ostensible ones. It seems that we had decided by summer to overthrow the Taliban, so we might have been waiting for some new terrorist act that would provide the immediate justification and might have done less to prevent this than we might otherwise. We were less interested in bringing Osama bin Laden to justice than in destroying the terrorist bases. Probably our policies were dictated as much by our desire for access to Caspian oil as to punish terrorists. None of this may affect our judgment about the justice of the war, but it should guide our thinking about the wider context.

If we make the uncertain supposition that the war against Afghanistan was just, does that make the overall war against terrorism just? Here, I think, the answer is a more emphatic no. It is an open-ended war without clear goals. There has been no definition of the terrorism that is to be eliminated. One suspects that we are committed to destroying only terror directed against us and that we do not plan to abandon the use of terror against others. For example, we continue to support terrorist groups in Latin America when they are supporting our policies there.

Consider the recent act of terrorism by Pakistanis against India. Does that justify the invasion of Pakistan by India as the act against us justified the invasion of Afghanistan? If so, are we committed to joining India in this attack? Fortunately, we are not reasoning in this way, even though some of our rhetoric would call for it. Because we want Pakistan as an ally, and because an attack on Pakistan would be met by fierce resistance and perhaps nuclear attack, our diplomacy calls for mediation, not war. Clearly we do not plan to go to war against all terrorists. The war on terrorism will be carried out selectively to suppress opposition to our global hegemony and to justify the most hawkish tendencies in U.S. foreign policy.

Christians who are not pacifists find it hard to speak clearly on war, yet surely this is a matter of great concern. As a process theologian, I do not see how we can avoid judging wars individually while realizing how very easy it is to rationalize our own nation's prejudices. I believe that the open-ended declaration of war against terrorism is providing a context in which our nation will pursue its narrowly nationalistic foreign policy with the constant threat of military force. It will intensify anger at us at least throughout the Muslim world. It is already being used to justify repressive tactics at home and abroad, and we can foresee that this situation will worsen. We should declare vigorously that this war is profoundly unjust. We should be prepared to make, in opposition to it, the kinds of sacrifices that Christian pacifists make in their opposition to war in general.